DEDICATION

As always, dedicated to my sweetheart (and now husband!) Stuart Schulman for believing in me until I believed in myself. I'm so lucky.

HEARTFELT THANKS TO:

- My publisher Karen Cooper for suggesting me for the project
- My editor Ross Weissman for his excellent author-management skills, brilliant pep talks, and awesome sense of humor
- The lovely Diane Gilleland of CraftyPod.com for writing the foreword
- My dear friend Beth Dunn for working some magic
- My husband Stuart Schulman for helping me like crazy with the lighting projects and anything that required a hand drill

CONTENTS

FOREWORD
Diane Gilleland, creator of CraftyPod.com

Ah, the humble Mason jar—a wholly useful thing that also manages to be beautiful. Why do we crafters love them so much? Is it that classic blocky shape? Their comforting heft? The charming embossed lettering? Or is it our memories (or ideals) of cozy kitchens and days spent putting by the summer garden yield for winter?

I've always loved the way Mason jars seem to materialize just as little household problems present themselves, offering perfect little solutions. I have a Mason jar in my kitchen that guards the aroma of my freshly roasted coffee beans. I have six more in my craft cabinet, keeping my buttons sorted by color. One on my back porch collaborates with a tea light and a little sand to form a lantern. And there's one in my toolbox, holding a motley assortment of nails and screws.

But you don't need to think of the Mason jar as "all-work-no-play." It also possesses creative potential. Mason jars love to mess around with paint and glitter and fabric and Mod Podge. They like taking part in holiday celebrations, brightening up windowsills, or even transforming themselves into light fixtures and travel cups. Best of all, no matter how much crafty re-tooling you give a Mason jar, it'll still end up being something useful. Which, to my mind, is the best kind of craft project— one that makes your life a little easier and a little more beautiful at the same time.

And this is where my friend Melissa Averinos comes in. She's the perfect person to write a book about Mason jar crafts. She's super-talented, but like the jars themselves, she won't hold you to impossible standards of creative perfection. She's more like a crafty buddy who encourages you to cozy up to the table, pours you a cup of tea, and doesn't freak out if you spill your paint. Her designs have the same warm, inviting quality that Mason jars do, and she's come up with a truly charming collection of projects that explore all their functional and decorative possibilities.

There's something special about a useful handmade item—it somehow carries the imprint of those delightful hours you spent making it, and it gives you back a little dose of that joy each time you use it.

. . . And now if you'll excuse me, I have a box of Mason jars in my garage that have a very bright future.

INTRODUCTION

Your pantry and fridge are stocked with them and you've got a drawer filled with regular and wide-mouth lids and screw bands.

But the Mason jar is much more than a container for soups and sauces, for canned applesauce and homemade jams and jellies. What you'll find in this book is some outside-of-the-jam-kitchen thinking. Of course, I love homemade pickles and jam with their pretty little labels—who doesn't? But I want to show you all the awesome possibilities that Mason jars offer the intrepid crafter; no sterilization required!

In this book you'll find thirty-five unique projects featuring Mason jars—everything from light fixtures to a tiered candy dish. All of them can brighten your home, whether it's the kitchen, the living room, or the bedroom. Although some of the projects are a bit more involved than others, none of them requires any more expertise than you have.

What You'll Need

All the supplies called for in these projects are readily available, either through your friendly local craft store, at a hardware or home improvement center, or lying around your house, just waiting to be used in a creative way. The most important things you'll need (apart from the Mason jars themselves) include:

- Permanent markers (like Sharpies) in assorted colors
- A power drill and bits (because some of the projects call for drilling holes in jar lids)
- Spray paint
- Mod Podge (if you've never used it, this is a glue, sealer, and finish—great for all kinds of craft projects)
- Glitter (all colors, shapes, and sizes—finally, an opportunity to put your glitter stash to use!)

Of course, many of the projects call for other supplies as well. Get creative and find supplies from your own home—objects that have been sitting in a closet or a drawer or in the attic. The more you personalize your Mason jar projects—make them connected to you and your family—the more you'll love them.

This leads me to another point: Don't feel that you need to follow the directions to the letter for the projects in this book. They're just a starting point. If you feel like altering or improving upon them, be my guest. Perhaps they'll inspire you to think of other ways to use Mason jars. Great! Go for it! That's what creativity is all about.

How to Use This Book

I've divided this book into five sections. The first, "Mason Miscellany," gives you some background about Mason jars and how they came to be a part of our lives. The other four—"In the Kitchen," "Around the Home," "Fun and Festivities," and "Useful Jars"—show how widely you can use your Mason jars for craft projects. Some of these projects call for more crafting than others. The projects that are part of the

"Useful Jars" section, however, won't require you to do much actual crafting to the jars. But don't let that stop you if you feel like adding some glitter or ribbons or spray paint to one of these projects. As I said, this is just a starting point.

I've also included an Appendix at the back of the book that contains art templates for some of the projects (these are referenced in the text) as well as some labels for you to photocopy and use as you like.

The most important thing you can do with this book is have fun. So go to it! Make some Mason jar magic!

PART 1

Mason Miscellany

Mason jars live a thousand lives. For ages, they've served as the most helpful of vessels; they're vehicles for preserving the tastes—and nutrition—of summer throughout the fall and winter months. Currently they're experiencing a resurgence as the darlings of crafters and wedding planners everywhere.

Honestly, though. It's just a glass jar with a screw-top lid. Right?

There's a lot more to Mason jars than meets the eye. They have a subtle genius that you only discover with time and persistence. You can freeze them, bake in them, or store food in them for months. The simple alchemy of glass, rubber, and metal somehow combines to produce a miracle of utility and panache that is unrivaled in the kitchen and pantry.

Small wonder, then, that we've started taking them into practically every other room in the house, using them for every conceivable purpose.

A Brief History of Mason Jars

Simple canning jars have been around at least since Napoleon uttered his famous dictum that "an army marches on its stomach." By 1810 a Frenchman, Nicholas Appert, had produced a recognizable version of today's canning jar just in time for Napoleon's plans for conquering most of the world. Then in 1858 an American tinsmith named John Landis Mason patented his own version of the jar, lending his name to a vastly improved edition featuring a threaded jar mouth, a rubber seal, and a reusable screw-on zinc cover.

The spread of the popular Mason jar owed a fair bit to the decision in 1886 by the Ball Brothers of Buffalo, New York, to manufacture the design. If the name "Ball" is ringing a bell, that's because "Ball jar" is to this day used interchangeably with "Mason jar" to indicate the common canning jar—and that's because so many of them came with the name "Ball" imprinted on the side during the final decades of the nineteenth century.

Alexander Kerr managed to improve on the sealing mechanism in 1903. He also gave the jar a much wider mouth, making it far easier to fill and decant. The new design was adopted by the Ball brothers, to immediate acclaim.

What Makes a Mason Jar a Mason Jar?

It's got to have a lid sealed with a rubber ring instead of wax. This innovation elevates a regular old canning jar to a true Mason jar. It doesn't matter what name is on the side (or if there's a name at all); if the lid has a rubber gasket and is fastened on with a threaded screw-top, you've got a Mason jar on your hands.

For readers of this book, it's important to know that Mason jars still come in two standard mouth widths:

1. The standard "regular mouth" has an opening of $2\frac{3}{8}$ inches across.
2. Kerr's "wide-mouth" version offers a more luxurious opening of 3 inches.

the basics:
regular mouth jars

HALF
PINT

regular mouth

PINT

regular mouth

QUART

regular mouth

and their
wide-mouth
counterparts

HALF
PINT
wide mouth

PINT

wide mouth

QUART

wide mouth

specialty shapes and sizes

4 oz.
JELLY JAR

regular mouth

HALF PINT

wide mouth

12 oz.
JELLY
JAR

regular mouth

HALF
GALLON

wide mouth

PINT
and a
HALF

wide mouth

PINT

wide mouth

As well, Mason jars come in a bewildering array of shapes and sizes, including the half-pint, pint, pint-and-a-half, quart, and half-gallon. It can be confusing at first, but you'll get the hang of it.

Canning

Home canning (what we sometimes refer to as "putting up" food for the winter) is the purpose for which Mason jars were first invented. You can cook or pickle your food first, pour it into your Mason jars, seal them, and set the food aside for colder days. Canning food can be a tricky undertaking, as it's important to sterilize the jars both before and during the procedure, so as to kill any organisms or enzymes that might seep in later and spoil the contents. Heating the jars after filling them also removes oxygen, which causes the vacuum that keeps food fresh for months.

Home canning became particularly popular during World War II, when people were growing their own vegetables in Victory Gardens.

After the war, even though people canned less, Mason jars came into their own.

Although they weren't being used to store food anymore, people didn't throw them away. The post-war generation started getting creative at finding other uses for the ubiquitous glass vessels. They used the jars for everything from drinking sweet tea on the front porch to keeping nuts and bolts sorted and handy in the work shed out back.

Mason jars never really fell out of fashion. Like all the great design objects, they just evolved.

Mason Jars Today

Today Mason jars are undergoing yet another revival. Young urban gardeners are rediscovering the rooftop garden (no, they didn't invent it) and using Mason jars to can their carefully tended heirloom tomatoes. The DIY community has discovered that Mason jars can be recruited to all manner of duties, including dry goods storage, decoration, and organization. Foodies and farmers' markets are featuring their best offerings in Mason jars as a way of signaling the virtues of small-batch, hand-crafted goods. Nearly every trend you can think of today that invokes the mantra "reduce, reuse, recycle" has some place in it for Mason jars.

Modern-day hackers are expanding the uses and possibilities for Mason jars by producing any number of innovations. You can grow a garden in a Mason jar, make one into a bird feeder, customize your very own travel mug, and fashion a lamp out of one.

In short, Mason jars have captured our imaginations—maybe even our hearts. They've seeped inescapably into our shared visual vocabulary and taken root as a symbol of simplicity, solidity, and self-sufficiency. You can see them in everything from wedding blogs to modern décor magazines. You can use them to provide a note of unpretentious country charm just as easily as a sturdy, glamour-free industrial edge. The humble canning jar has come a long way since it campaigned with Napoleon across the steppes of Russia, and it's surely got a long way to go before we're done with it.

PART 2

In the Kitchen

Of course, the kitchen is where you'd expect to find Mason jars. What you may not expect is to see them painted bright colors, decorated in interesting and imaginative ways, and performing a variety of functions—everything from a straw tumbler to a salad dressing mixer.

I find that having these handmade objects in my kitchen inspires me to be more creative with my cooking and makes me smile to boot.

MASON
SALAD DRESSING MIXER

homemade
salad dressing
is yummy

you will Need:

- Measuring cup and water

- Pint-size Kerr brand Mason jar with three smooth sides (I specify Kerr here because most Ball jars have embossing on all sides, which makes them undesirable for this project)

- Sharpie permanent markers in an assortment of colors and tip sizes

Sometimes I get lazy and use store-bought salad dressing, but the homemade kind tastes so much better. This quick project provides a great starting point for creating your own. Homemade salad dressing will generally keep two weeks in the fridge, but it's so yummy that in my house it rarely lasts that long.

1. Measure ¾ cup of water and pour into the jar. Set the jar on an even surface. Using the marker on a non-embossed side of the jar, mark a dot at the waterline. Add ¼ cup more water. Mark a dot at the new water level. Empty the jar and make sure the outside is dry before continuing.

2. Draw a horizontal line about 2 inches wide at each dot. Don't worry if it's a little wiggly. You can always practice on a pickle jar if this makes you nervous. If you *really* don't like what you have drawn on the glass, take it off with some acetone nail polish remover and a cotton ball.

3. Under (or next to) the bottom line, write "oil" and under (or next to) the top line write "vinegar." These measurements will give you an easy vinaigrette base from which to make your own dressing.

CRAFTY HINT

To make your salad dressing mix jar more decorative, use some Sharpies to draw carrots or other decorative veggies on the jar. They'll remind you of what a healthy meal you're preparing.

Use some of my ideas to decorate the rest of the jar, or come up with your own. Have fun with it! To make the marks more permanent and set the ink, you can bake the jar in a home oven. Preheat the oven to 350°F. Place the jar on a baking sheet and put it in the oven for 30 minutes. Allow the jar to cool for a while before removing it from the oven with oven mitts.

Mason Musings

Creating your own salad dressing recipes is super fun because you can just improvise with whatever you have on hand. You can't go wrong, starting out with oil and vinegar. Your new salad dressing jar automatically gives you a 3-to-1 proportion, but if you know you like a different ratio, feel free to adjust the measurements for your own jar. I like to use extra virgin olive oil and balsamic vinegar, but you might prefer something else.

For something savory try adding one of these: a pinch of dried herbs or a bunch of fresh; a tablespoon of your favorite prepared mustard or plain yogurt (which helps to emulsify the dressing so it stays mixed rather than immediately separating into oil and vinegar layers); or a tablespoon of something strongly flavored such as sesame oil, fresh minced ginger, or fresh minced garlic. When they are in season, I smash a handful of fresh-picked raspberries in mine.

For something sweet, try: a tablespoon of honey, brown rice syrup, agave nectar, or maple syrup.

And, of course, salt and freshly cracked pepper to taste.

QUIRKY CHEESE SHAKERS

it's wicked easy
but it looks
fancypants.

p.s.
herbs mixed in
are yummy

mmmmm, cheese.

You Will Need:

- Pint-size Mason jar
- Permanent marker
- Drill press (if you don't have a drill press, you can use a hand drill or hammer and nail)

This quick project makes a charming cheese shaker that looks way cuter on the dinner table than those plastic containers you're used to using! It's also perfect for powdered sugar at brunch.

1. Separate the lid from the jar and mark where you want the holes to be on the top of the lid. You can use as many or as few as you like. Of course, the more holes you have, the more cheese will come out when you shake it. Mmmmm. Cheese.

2. Using the drill press, make holes at the markings. A drill press works best because it doesn't leave burrs (sharp bits of metal).

3. If you don't have a drill press, use a hand drill as follows: Drill pilot holes with a small bit, then enlarge the holes using a ¼-inch bit. If there are sharp edges on the underside of the lid, file as needed to make it smooth. If you don't have a hand drill either, use a hammer and nails of increasing sizes to get the holes to about ¼ inch across. Make sure you use a block of scrap wood under the lid as you hammer the nail. File the underside of the lid as necessary, using a metal file (or sandpaper if you don't have a file).

fewer holes:

more holes:

less cheese per shake

more cheese per shake

obviously this is the way to go

4. Wash the lid thoroughly to remove any metal shavings. Fill the jar with grated parmesan, replace the lid, and screw on the band.

This makes an awesome hostess gift when paired with a loaf of bread from a local bakery and wrapped with a pretty tea towel. Just a little heads up in case you are feeling lazy—you can totally fake this project if you have a plastic shaker of parm in your fridge. Try that green lid on a regular-mouth Mason jar—the caps on many brands fit perfectly!

Mason Musings

Here's a chance to use your new cheese shaker *and* some of those fresh herbs you've been growing. Remember to chop the herbs fine enough that they will fit through the holes in the shaker.

CHEESE MIXTURE OF GREAT AWESOMENESS

8 ounces grated Parmesan-Romano mix of your liking
2 tablespoons fresh oregano, finely chopped
2 tablespoons fresh thyme, finely chopped
2 tablespoons fresh basil, finely chopped
1 teaspoon dried crushed red pepper
1 teaspoon dried garlic powder
½ teaspoon freshly ground black pepper (a few turns of the grinder, if you have one)

Mix all ingredients in a bowl. Adjust to taste (don't eat it all).

Use this little concoction just as you would plain grated cheese. Sprinkle liberally over pasta and sauce, shake it on pizza, or try it in your own homemade salad dressing (see the previous project for inspiration). This also makes a killer garlic bread: Just slice up a loaf of your favorite artisan bread, smear it with olive oil, and coat it with the Cheese Mixture of Great Awesomeness. Broil until it's toasty and yummy smelling. Nom.

CLASSIC STRAW TUMBLERS

perfect for a barbecue
or garden party

You Will Need:

- Pint-size Mason jar (or another size you would want to drink from, such as a regular-mouth half-pint jar)
- Ruler
- Permanent marker
- Block of scrap wood
- Power drill and bits
- Gloss enamel spray paint (optional)
- Cardboard (optional)
- Rubber grommet with ¼-inch diameter inner hole and ⁹⁄₁₆-inch outer diameter (available at hardware stores)
- Plastic straw (double-check to make sure your straw fits inside your grommet)

This simple project is perfect for use as an eco-friendly travel tumbler. You'll be all right if the drink sloshes while in your cupholder, but you might get a bit wet if the jar gets turned upside down. (Note: It's not watertight!)

1. Separate the lid from the band and set the band aside. Using your ruler, measure the diameter of the lid and mark a dot in the center with your permanent marker.

2. Place the lid right side up on the block of wood. Start with a small hole and gradually make the hole larger so the rubber grommet will fit. Using a ³⁄₁₆-inch bit, drill a pilot hole. (If you happen to have a drill press, you can skip the pilot hole, drill a ⁵⁄₁₆-inch opening, and move to step 4.)

3. Next, use a ¼-inch drill bit and drill into the pilot hole. Repeat with a ⁵⁄₁₆-inch bit. Now the hole should be just a hair larger than the opening of the grommet. Make sure the drilled hole is *not* larger than the grommet itself.

4. Thoroughly wash and dry the lid to remove any metal shavings left from drilling.

5. If you like, spray paint the lid and screw band a fun color! Lay them on cardboard outside and give them a couple of coats of paint, letting them dry in between. If you are making a bunch of tumblers, it would be cute to do the lids one color and the bands another.

6. Squeeze the grommet a little bit and place into the hole in the lid. It should spring right back out and fit within the hole. Move it around as necessary to get it to fit correctly.

7. Fill the jar with something delicious to drink and put the lid and screw band in place.

8. Pop your straw in and sip on the go!

everybody

LOVES

bendy straws

(it is a known fact)

Mason Musings

This is one of those projects that can be easily customized to suit any event or holiday, if you feel like getting your Martha on. Try color coordinating the straws with the lids, screw bands, and even the drink! Some examples to get you started:

- Valentine's Day: fruit punch, red-and-white striped straw, red band, pink lid
- Easter: pink lemonade, yellow-and-white striped straw, yellow band, pink lid
- Graduation party: use school colors
- Wedding: coordinate with the wedding colors or keep it simple with white and silver (or gold)
- Independence Day: blue Kool-Aid, blue-and-white striped straw, red band, white lid
- Halloween: orange soda, purple straw, black band, orange lid
- Thanksgiving: apple cider, orange straw, gold band, brown lid

Come up with some combinations for the winter holidays on your own.

TIERED TREAT STAND

spray-paint with gloss enamel if you like

glue another plate at the bottom for three levels of treats

You Will Need:

* 2 Mason jars (one 4-ounce jelly jar, 1 wide-mouth half-pint jar)

* 2 glass dishes (plate or shallow bowl, one 6½ inches and one 4½ inches in diameter)

* E6000 adhesive (available at craft and hardware stores)

Make your own multilevel sweets tray out of Mason jars paired with glass dishes. They are perfect for candy or mini-cupcakes, but they could also be used as an alternative to a traditional cheese and cracker plate if made in a larger size.

1. Disassemble the jars and set the lids and screw bands aside for another project. Thoroughly wash and dry the jars if they are not brand new, right from the package. Pair your jars and dishes together as they will be glued for each tier.

2. When working with nonporous surfaces such as glass, it's best to put the adhesive on both surfaces, let them sit for a minute, and then join them. First apply a ring of the glue around the bottom outside of the jar. Place the jar on a steady surface, glue side up. Grasping both sides of the plate or bowl, center the bottom of the dish over the jar and gently press onto the bottom of the jar—then pull it away. Use the glue left behind on the plate as a guide for adding more adhesive. Only glue in a ring; you don't need to glue the whole surface inside the ring.

3. After you let both pieces sit for a minute, carefully re-center the plate over the jar and press firmly. Let sit for a day or until the glue is completely dry. Repeat with the other pair.

Once both sets are dry, glue the smaller tier to the larger tier. Let them dry and fill them with wrapped confections.

Take care not to let unwrapped food come in contact with the dried glue where the tiers are joined. Tie a ribbon around the join or cover the glue discreetly with plastic wrap. Trust me, nobody is going to notice when that thing is piled high with goodies!

E6000 is an industrial-strength glue, so the bond will be pretty secure, but you still want to be gentle with your treat stand. To clean it, simply wipe it with a damp cloth and let it air-dry.

INDUSTRIAL STRENGTH

E6000

E6000 adhesive is a great addition to your crafty arsenal.

use on
*glass
*wood
*metal
*ceramics

Mason Musings

I love a doily-topped cake stand heaped with cookies or a little pedestal bearing a cupcake. Instead of (or in addition to) making the tiered stand, try leaving each jar and plate combo as individual stands. Make several in different heights and sizes for a killer appetizer display at your next gathering. Audition different combinations of plates and jars. Once you have decided on the pairings you like, go for it!

Use as is—without the lid on the base jar—or gently turn the stand over and fill the jar with something cute or pretty and use the lid and band to seal the contents inside. Vary the decorative jar fillings according to the event or what you will be using the stands for, such as:

- Easter: cello grass with Jordan almonds or Marshmallow Peeps for a treat stand filled with deviled eggs
- Christmas: vintage glass ornaments and a plate of cookies for Santa
- Valentine's Day: pink-and-red M&M's with cupcakes

Use your imagination and have fun with it!

CHALKBOARD PANTRY JARS

chalkboard labels: the awesomeness cannot be denied

You Will Need:

- Black chalkboard paint (either paint-on or spray)
- Black construction paper
- Scissors
- Decorative edge scissors
- Hole punch (optional)
- Rubber cement
- Mason jars with at least one smooth (non-embossed) side, as many as you like
- Chalk, chalk pencils, or chalkboard markers

When chalkboard paint became readily available, I was obsessed. Since then, I have calmed down a bit, but I'm still crazy about chalkboards. This project is a fun introduction to the joys of making things write-on-able. It's also a great way to showcase your Mason jars.

1. Paint or spray the black construction paper with the chalkboard paint and let it dry completely. Repeat twice for good coverage. You just made chalkboard paper!

2. Decide what shape and size you want the chalkboard area to be on your jar. Get creative with it and think outside of a rectangle. Want to have a decorative edge on the sides? Use your fancy-pants scrapbooking scissors, the ones with a scalloped edge, to cut out a piece of the chalkboard paper. Rifle through your craft supplies and see if you have some hole punchers in different sizes. Use them to make little polka dots along the edge of the chalkboard label.

3. Carefully apply rubber cement to the back of the paper and apply the label to the smooth side of the jar. After positioning the label, rub along the edge with your fingernail to make sure the whole label is adhered to the jar. Let it dry and rub away any leftover rubber cement.

4. Rub a piece of chalk over the chalkboard surface and rub it in with your fingers, then wipe away any remaining chalk. This will dull the surface a bit and make it better for writing and erasing chalk. Now fill the jars with your pantry staples, grab some chalk, and write the contents on the chalkboard. Experiment with chalk pencils or chalkboard markers, both available at craft stores.

CRAFTY HINT

You can use more than a basic stick of chalk to write on these jars. One of my favorite ways to mark on chalkboards is with gouache paint, which is an opaque watercolor. You can get this at art supply and craft stores, either in cake form or in tubes. Using a fine brush, paint a pretty border on the chalkboard or use it to write the contents.

If you aren't comfortable with painting, experiment with chalkboard markers, available at craft stores.

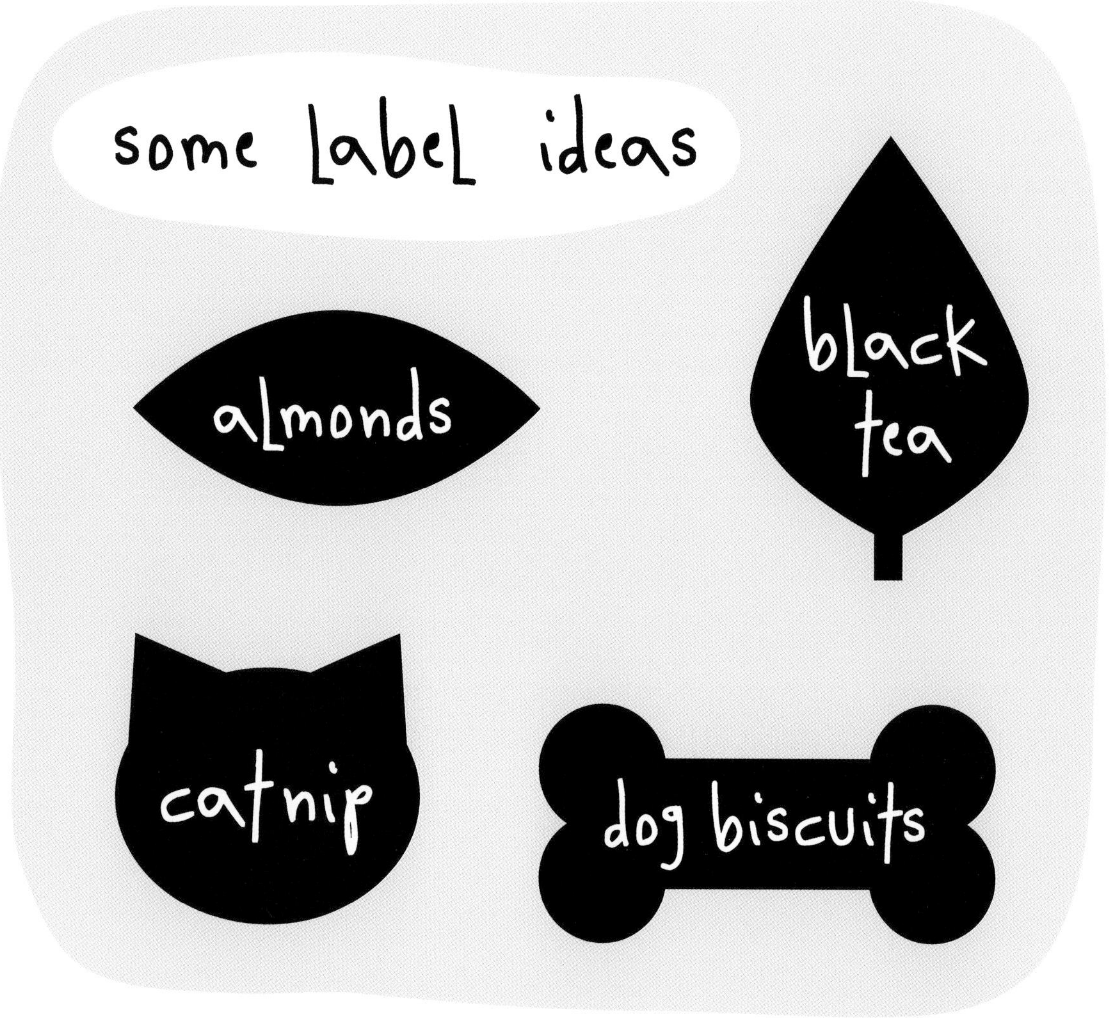

some label ideas

almonds

black tea

catnip

dog biscuits

WASHI TAPE UTENSIL JARS

washi jar
+
spoon makeover
=
adorable kitchen

You Will Need:

- Washi tape in assorted sizes, colors, and prints
- Scissors
- Quart-size Mason jar—the totally smooth kind made especially for crafting

What's more kitchen-y than a Mason jar? Quart-size canning jars make the perfect utensil holders and are totally customizeable to your taste. Get crafty washi tape and you've got a cute kitchen essential for a fraction of the price you'd pay at Big Box Kitchen Emporium.

1. Play with your rolls of washi tape until you find an arrangement you like. You can alternate solids, subtle patterns, and busy patterns, as well as the space between them.

2. Once you have an idea of how you would like to apply the tape, cut your washi tape into 12½-inch strips and apply one at a time to the jar. Leave the bottom inch or so of curvy jar and the top few inches of curvy jar free from tape. Otherwise, it's hard to get the tape nice and smooth. Overlap the tape strips at the same spot, which we will consider "the back," and place the jar against the counter's backsplash!

3. I like to fold up a paper towel and put it at the bottom of the jar to absorb any drips when I'm putting away wet dishes. Place your cutest or your most often-used utensils in the jar and set it on the kitchen counter. If you like to have all your stuff out where you can see it, perhaps

you'll want to make a set—one for your rubber spatulas,
one for wooden spoons, one for . . . well, you get the idea.
These are great for craft room storage, too!

CRAFTY HINT

Once I had my adorable jar, I had to make my wooden spoon collection a little bit sassy.

Use painter's tape to block off a few inches down from the spoon part—you don't want paint on the part of the spoon that will come in contact with food. Paint the rest of the handle with white primer like Kilz 2. Once it dries, paint it with a bright color enamel paint. Enamel is nice and hard, but if you don't have it, you can use several coats of artist's acrylic and then add a sealing coat of a water-based varnish like Minwax Polycrylic. The more spoons and colors you have, the cuter it looks! Or you can go with several spoons painted the same color, maybe one of the colors of your washi tape. Put all your spoons in your washi jar and admire your quick project. Adorable, right?

MASON MAGNETS

use my reminders or make your own

mmmm, Brussels sprouts

take some deep breaths

eat your veggies

go for a run

chug some water

you = awesome

you'll feel better if you do

call a friend

true story

You Will Need:

- Lids left over from other projects
- Newspaper or scrap cardboard
- Spray primer
- Acrylic or craft paint
- Waxed paper
- Craft paintbrush
- Paper towel or damp cloth
- Photocopies of the designs in the Appendix
- Craft glue
- Spray gloss sealer or Mod Podge (optional)
- Watercolors, permanent markers, colored pencils (optional)
- 1-inch craft magnets
- Hot glue gun

After doing just a few of these Mason jar projects you are bound to have a bunch of lids hanging around. Use them to make refrigerator magnets that bear reminders we all need from time to time.

1. Take the lids outside and lay them, shiny side up, on some newspaper or cardboard. Give them an even coat of spray primer. Let them dry and repeat until the lids are white. If you don't have spray primer lying around, you can brush on artist's gesso or a water-based household primer such as Kilz 2. (I love that stuff, and I always try to keep a gallon around because I use it for everything.)

2. Once the lids are primed, it's time to add a little bit of paint. You can use your favorite colors or you may choose to coordinate the magnets with your kitchen décor. You could leave them white, too. If you decide to go with color, dab a bit of acrylic paint on the waxed paper and mix it with a wet brush. The brush will add some water to thin out the paint so it will be translucent. If you prefer the color to be opaque, mix it with a dry brush.

3. Paint the lids. For a less uniform look, use a paper towel or damp cloth to dab away some of the paint. Play around with it until you like how it looks. Let the lids dry completely.

4.   Paint the designs from the Appendix with water-colors or use colored pencils or markers to add color.

5.   If you're feeling lazy, photocopy the designs onto different-colored papers or leave them white like I did. Cut out just inside the dotted line. Smear the back with craft glue and stick designs to the centers of the lids. Let them dry.

6.   If you like, spray a coat of gloss sealer or brush on a coat of Mod Podge to protect the surface and give it a shine. Or maybe you prefer a matte finish, in which case matte Mod Podge will work like a dream. Let the lids dry. (If you're feeling snazzy you can glue on some little gems or buttons along the outside of your magnets.)

7.   Turn over the lids and glue on the magnets with the hot glue gun. Let the glue dry. Put the magnets on the fridge where you will be reminded daily to eat your veggies, call your mother, let it go, drink some water, or go for a run. I don't know about you, but I need all the reminders I can get. Of course, I encourage you to come up with your own meaningful reminders if you prefer!

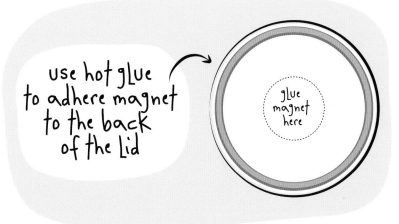

use hot glue to adhere magnet to the back of the lid

glue magnet here

HOMESPUN SOAP DISPENSER

coolest soap dispenser ever

you could
use it for
ketchup
and
mustard,
too

you will Need:

- Pint-size Mason jar
- Ruler
- Permanent marker
- Block of scrap wood
- Power drill and bits
- Needle-nosed pliers
- Soap dispenser pump (you can take the pump from an inexpensive soap dispenser or just use one that you already have)
- Utility knife
- Hot glue gun
- A piece of scrap cardboard

A charming addition to your bathroom or kitchen, this liquid soap dispenser fits in with just about any décor. You could make an extra one and fill it with your favorite hand lotion for a matched set.

1. Separate the lid from the band and set the band aside. Using your ruler, measure the diameter of the lid and mark a dot in the center with your permanent marker.

2. Place the lid right side up on the block of wood. Using a ³⁄₁₆-inch bit, drill a pilot hole.

3. Next, use a slightly larger drill bit and drill into the pilot hole. Repeat with larger drill bits until the hole starts to approach the size of the pump tube. Do not make the hole too big! (Ideally, you would work up to a drill bit of the exact width of the pump tube. I didn't have the right size, and you may not either. No big deal.)

4. Grab your pliers and keep them closed. Put them through the hole in the lid and apply a little bit of pressure as you twist to widen the hole a tiny bit. Keep checking the fit of the pump tube every few turns. You want it to be snug so take your time and widen the hole in small increments. Don't fret; it's not an exact science. If you end up with a hole that the tube fits into, then you did it right.

5. Once the tube fits snugly into the lid, hold the pump next to the jar with the lid level with where it will rest, once assembled with the jar. You will probably see that the "straw" part of the pump extends beyond the bottom of the jar. You need to trim it with your utility knife, so it will fit inside the jar. It should come to ½ inch from the bottom of the jar.

cut the pump tube so it's ½" from the bottom of the jar

6. Separate the pump from the lid and thoroughly wipe down each part to remove any metal bits or shavings left from drilling.

7. Lift the collar up and away from the lid a little bit and squeeze some hot glue under the collar. Quickly press the pump back into place and hold it for a few moments until the glue cools.

8. Fill the jar with your favorite liquid hand soap and put the lid and band in place. If you forgo the glue in step 7, you can use this design for ketchup and mustard dispensers at a cookout.

PART 3

Around the Home

Of course, we all have the odd Mason jar collecting pens on the desk, but Mason jars have many more uses outside the kitchen than just holding pens and pencils. Whether you need a new pincushion for your sewing projects or want to make over the lighting in your living room, you'll see that Mason jars can provide a solution to almost any problem around the home.

PINCUSHION

if you like,
decorate the
felt with buttons
or rickrack

You Will Need:

- Quart-size Mason jar
- 4" × 4" square of card stock
- Pencil
- 5" × 5" cotton fabric scrap
- Poly batting, available at fabric and craft stores
- Hot glue gun
- 7½" × 12¾" piece of felt
- 3 straight pins
- Sewing machine (needle and thread if you want to hand sew)

Mason jar pincushions have been around for ages and I can see why. It's a clever and utilitarian project that has the side benefit of being adorable. What's not to love?

This craft room staple gets an update with an attached tool belt caddy. It's like a cute little apron for your tools!

1. Separate the lid and band from the jar. Using the lid as a template, trace a circle on the card stock and cut it about ¼ inch inside to make a circle that is smaller than the lid. You will later glue this piece onto the underside of the lid to hide the glued-on fabric. If you prefer, you can use an additional piece of felt for this instead of card stock. Just trace your circle with chalk instead of pencil.

2. Lay the screw band upside down on a table and lay the cotton fabric face down over it. Ball up a handful of batting and lay it on the center of the fabric. Pick it all up and gently push some of the batting and fabric through the hole of the band to start to form the pincushion. Make sure you don't push it all the way through!

3. Holding the edge of the fabric against the band, stuff a bit more batting into the fabric until you create a firm

rounded cushion that comes out from the top of the screw band. Pull the fabric taut and smooth out any wrinkles in the top of the cushion.

4. Once you have the cushion looking nice and uniform, carefully glue the fabric to the underside of the lid with your glue gun. Glue your piece of felt in place to cover up the fabric.

5. Squish the stuffing toward the middle, to relieve a little bit of the puffiness from the edge of the cushion. You don't want it to be too thick at the edges or you won't be able to screw the band on over it.

6. Now to make the caddy part. Fold the felt as shown in the diagram. Place three pins evenly spaced across the width of the folded-over part, and sew at the pins as shown, making sure to backstitch for a good ½ inch at the opening of the pocket. Backstitch a few stitches at the bottom to finish. Fold with the right sides (pocket side) together and using a ¼-inch seam allowance, stitch the edges together to make a tube. Turn the tube right side out and slip it onto the Mason jar. It should be nice and snug like a cozy. Fill with your tracing wheel, disappearing ink pens, and whatnot. Now go sew something cute!

12.75"

4.5"

fold up 3"

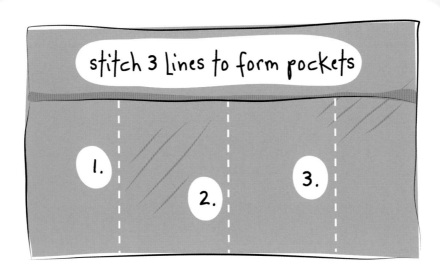

stitch 3 lines to form pockets

1. 2. 3.

CLOUD JARS

some spray paint and painter's tape is
all you need to make these cute cloud jars

You Will Need:

- Roll of 2-inch-wide blue painter's tape
- Fine-tip permanent marker
- Scissors
- 1 quart Mason jar and 1 pint Mason jar with some smooth, non-embossed areas (I like the Kerr brand for this project)
- Cardboard
- Sky-blue enamel spray paint
- X-ACTO knife or razor blade

A bright blue sky with puffy white clouds always brings a smile to my face. Bring that cheerful vision inside and turn ordinary bathroom essentials into happy clouds.

1. With the tape still on the roll, draw a cloud shape on the masking tape with your marker. I like to make my clouds with overlapping circles—a cluster of five or so on the bottom, and three medium ones in the middle, with the two on the outside smaller. Then I draw two medium circles on the top sides and a large one on the top middle, slightly off-center. Clouds are irregular, so don't get too caught up in being perfect about it.

2. Make as many or as few clouds as you like. I like to vary the sizes, but it's perfectly okay to have a more uniform look. Continue drawing clouds until you reach the beginning of the roll of tape.

3. Snip off one cloud and carefully cut out along the marked line. The sticky side of the tape will try to grab your scissors, so just take your time and practice patience.

4. Once you have a cloud cut out, choose a smooth, non-embossed spot on the jar to place your first cloud. I like to start at the front and place the clouds near the lettering so that when the jar sits on my shelf I can see the cotton balls or cotton swabs through the clouds on the front of the jar.

5. Gently press the center of the tape cloud onto the glass. Starting at the middle of the cloud, press all around the tape to smooth it out and adhere it to the jar. Rub with your fingernail around the edges to get a nice seal, so no paint seeps in.

6. Repeat steps 3–5 to draw, cut out, and adhere as many clouds as necessary for each jar. I like smaller clouds for the front to fit around the lettering and larger clouds for the sides and back of the jar.

7. Now you are ready to spray-paint. Lay some cardboard outside on a flat surface. Place the jars mouth-down on the cardboard and spray-paint both of them completely. Make sure you use even strokes and try not to linger in one place too long or drips will develop. Let the jars dry completely and give them a second coat.

8. Once the second coat of spray paint is completely dry, gently grasp the edge of a tape cloud and slowly peel away from the jar, revealing the clear glass beneath it. Repeat for all of the clouds. Use the blade to carefully scrape off any paint that seeped beneath the masking tape.

Fill the shorter jar with cotton swabs and the taller jar with cotton balls. It's your choice whether to use the lids and screw bands or not. If you do want to use them, you can leave them metallic or spray paint them white or blue to match.

CRAFTY HINT

These are not waterproof and they *will* scratch if you drag your fingernail across them, so don't. If you want to make them slightly more scratch-resistant, you can use a spray primer first, follow with two or three coats of the blue spray paint, and finish with a clear gloss top coat.

how to draw clouds

circles

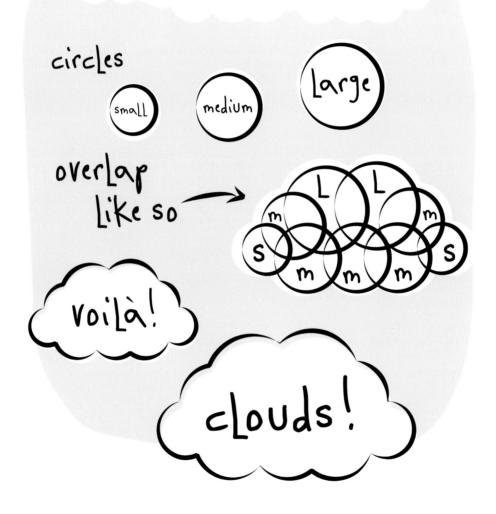

overlap
like so →

voilà!

clouds!

PASTEL DISTRESSED JARS

pretty
vintage
pastel
awesome

You Will Need:

- Mason jars
- Cardboard
- Spray primer
- Spray paint
- Sandpaper

Charming pastels get some tough love by way of sandpaper. This project would work equally well with bright colors or even neutrals. Coordinate the colors with your décor and use these distressed jars as pretty storage or purely ornamental pieces. Or for a little bit of both worlds, pop a votive in each one and you've got some unique candleholders.

1. Disassemble the jars and set aside the lids and screw bands. Thoroughly wash and dry the jars.

2. Lay the jars outside on cardboard. I find it easier to spray-paint when I can walk around the item, so you might want to try setting up a milk crate with cardboard on it, to create a "stand."

3. Place the jars mouth down and slowly spray the primer in an even coat all over the jars.

4. Let primer dry and then repeat with the color spray paint. Let the jars dry and repeat if necessary to get total coverage. Try not to spray too close or for too long in one spot or you will get drips.

5. Once the jars are dry, rub sandpaper all over the paint. I like to think of it as smoothing the paint rather than trying to sand it off—better to go lightly over it several times than to take too much off at once. Sand as much or as little as you want to get the amount of "distress" you prefer.

use sandpaper to create the level of distress you prefer

more   less

If you are going to use these as storage jars, and you don't like the look of the metal covers, prime and paint the lid and screw band. You can leave the paint as is or distress it as you did the jar. Fill with your stuff and you are good to go.

If you like these for decorative purposes only, arrange them in a little vignette that pleases you. You might like to group them with items of the same color, or with some favorite things that have the same vibe. With flowers in them these would look great as the centerpieces for tables at a wedding!

CRAFTY HINT

Try different finishes. The basic gloss spray paint will give a semi-shiny finish. Try the new "for plastic" spray paints—they don't say so on the bottle, but these paints give you a matte, almost pebbly finish. Conversely, see what metallic gold or silver looks like after being roughed up a bit. Or, give the jars a coat or two of spray gloss sealer to bring out a high shine after you distress the paint. This has the fringe benefit of giving the jars a bit of protection from further, unintentional scratching.

VINTAGE CEILING LIGHT

perfect for a porch light

You Will Need:

* 1 quart Mason jar (you will not need the lid and screw band for this project, so save them for another project)

* Black electrical tape

* Scissors

* Flush-mounted or semi-flush ceiling light fixture

Could your boring old hall light use some sprucing up? This inexpensive lighting update will show off your home decorating skills. You can even use these instructions to replace an ugly globe on a ceiling fan light.

1. Carefully wrap the neck of the jar with electrical tape, pressing it with your fingers so it sticks in between the raised areas of the glass. Make sure to only come down as far as the screw band would cover, otherwise, you will see it when the light is installed.

press the electrical tape into the raised glass grooves

2. Wrap the tape around the mouth of the jar a second time to make a two-layer thickness. Snip the tape off the roll and press the end of the tape firmly to the jar.

CRAFTY HINT

In a pinch, duct tape will work just as well as electrical tape. You'll just have to cut it into one-inch strips first. Don't use masking tape, though, because it will dry out over time and possibly cause the glass to come loose from the fixture.

3. Turn the light off. You are not working with electricity or wiring here, so you don't have to worry about turning off any main power, but you should give the base and globe of your ceiling fixture time to cool before you touch them.

4. Remove the existing globe from your ceiling light fixture by loosening the screws on the sides of the base. Insert the Mason jar into place, making sure the tape is covered by the collar of the base. The glass jar may be thicker than the globe you are replacing, so if the screws are preventing you from putting the jar in place, loosen them first.

5. Tighten each screw until it just touches the jar enough to hold it up. Then go around again and tighten the screws some more until the jar is securely in place. Easy!

Mason Musings

Don't like your existing fixture *at all*, right down to the shiny faux-brass base? No problem! Take that ugly duckling down (using all safety precautions, of course, including turning off the electricity) and give it a good cleaning. Separate the screws from the base. Wrap them with painter's tape, leaving the heads exposed. Lay the screws and the ceiling light base on some cardboard outside and give them two good coats of spray primer. Follow with a few coats of glossy white spray paint or a color that coordinates with the room it lives in. Let dry. Reinstall your made-over light fixture base, add the Mason jar of your choice, and *bam*! Completely new ceiling light. Wow, you're crafty.

PENDANT LIGHTING

use a standard light bulb with wide-mouth jars

use a small flame-shaped bulb on regular-mouth jars

You Will Need:

- Replacement lighting fixture for a paper lantern (also called a "single-socket cord kit")
- Wide-mouthed pint Mason jar
- Foam core
- Pencil
- X-ACTO knife
- White screw-in hooks

Have you seen how expensive pendant lighting is these days? Save some cash and get some crafty satisfaction by transforming a paper lantern fixture and a Mason jar into a charming pendant light in just a few quick steps.

1. Turn off the power to the light you're working on.

2. Unscrew the band from the Mason jar and remove the lid. Using the lid as a template, trace a circle on the foam core. If you don't have any foam core, but you happen to have an expired political lawn sign made of corrugated plastic board, you can use that.

3. Cut out the circle about ⅛ inch inside the traced line with the X-ACTO knife. Of course, you will want to make sure you don't cut anything beneath the foam core, so put a couple layers of cardboard or a piece of scrap wood under it.

4. With your fingers, pinch the edge all around the foam core circle to flatten it a bit. This will make it possible for the band to fit over it and screw onto the jar.

5. Place the foam core disc inside the screw band where the lid would normally go, to see if it fits. It should be very snug. If it doesn't fit, carefully cut a little more away from the outside. If it is so loose that it slips through the big

hole in the top of the screw band, sorry, but you will have
to try again.

6. Unscrew the collar from the light fixture. Use the collar as a template to trace a new, smaller circle onto the center of your foam core circle. Cut carefully on the line this
time and remove the center. This leaves you with a ring.

7. Holding the light and the cord at the base, put the
screw band (top down, screw side up) over the light fixture
catch so it doesn't slide down the cord. Slide the foam core
ring onto the base of the light, where it will catch on the
lip of the base. Slide the screw band up and fit the foam
circle into it. The screw band and foam core ring should
now be firmly in place at the base of the light fixture.

8. Screw on the collar, insert the light bulb, and screw
on the jar. Attach the hooks and hang the cord from them.

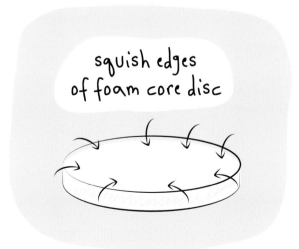

squish edges
of foam core disc

Mason Musings

Cluster multiple pendant lights together to create a gorgeous lighting piece that will be the envy of all of your friends. You can make three lights the same size and just vary the height at which they hang. Or, use this project as an opportunity to show off all the different-sized Mason jars you've been collecting. You can create a simple cluster of one small, one medium, and one large, or go all the way with as many as you like.

Keep in mind when making your jar choices that you need to use a light bulb that fits each jar. If you are using a tall and narrow 12-ounce jelly jar, you'll have to use a different shape and size bulb than you could use on a larger, wide-mouth jar. Also, it's probably best to limit the sizes you use to anything under a half gallon. Otherwise, there may be too much weight pulling on the cord. As always, experimentation is the name of the game.

MASON JAR OIL LAMP

trim wick down
if the flame
is too high

fill your jars with
ocean rocks
or
evergreens
(or whatever you like)

You Will Need:

- ½" wide cotton twill tape (or a cotton shoelace with the taped ends cut off, thick baker's twine, or any other kind of woven cord that is 100-percent cotton)

- Odorless paraffin lamp oil

- Mason jar, size and shape your choice

- Hand drill

- Ruler

- Permanent marker

The Internet says you can stop by a craft store and find a glass insert and fiberglass wick for making your own oil lamp. But it's just as much fun—and cheaper and more creative—to rig your own. That's right, I'm DIY-ing a DIY project. All you need is a Mason jar, some lamp oil, and something cotton to use as a wick.

1. Measure the diameter of the lid and mark a dot with the permanent marker in the center.

2. Drill a ⅛-inch hole where you marked the center of the lid. If there are sharp edges on the underside of the lid, file them as needed to make the lid smooth. If you don't have a hand drill, use a hammer and nails of increasing sizes to get the hole to about ⅛ inch across. Make sure you use a block of scrap wood under the lid as you hammer the nail. File the underside of the lid as necessary using a metal file (or sandpaper if you don't have a file).

3. Cut a length of twill tape (or whatever you are using for the wick) so it is twice the height of the jar you are using. From the underside of the lid, thread the "wick" through the hole so ½ inch protrudes from the top of the lid. It should be snug enough that the cord doesn't fall

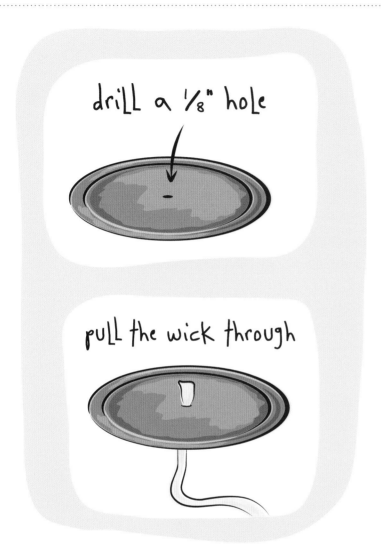

through the hole but loose enough that you can tug the material up to advance the wick when it burns down. You may have to double up your wick material or increase the size of the hole to make the fit right. Don't worry about it too much; you just need to make sure the wick doesn't fall through the hole.

4. Fill the jar with paraffin lamp oil. You can get decorative here, if you like. Before topping off with oil, place a bunch of pretty evergreens or beach stones in the jar. Once the jar is filled, place the lid and wick onto the mouth of the jar and secure with the screw band. Let the cotton soak up the oil for at least an hour before lighting the top portion of the wick. Of course, do not leave any flame burning unattended.

TIP:

Lamp oil is, obviously, flammable, so keep the lamp out of the reach of small children, pets, or anything else that might accidentally knock it over.

REED DIFFUSER

bamboo skewers

use your favorite
essential oils

You Will Need:

* 8-ounce jelly jar
* Sweet almond oil (available at natural food stores)
* Essential oils of your choice
* 15 thin bamboo skewers
* Scissors
* Rubbing alcohol or vodka
* Transparent Solo plastic cup or something similar
* Lighter
* X-ACTO knife

Scent is an easily overlooked element in creating a mood in a room. We focus on the wall color, the lighting, the music we listen to . . . but how about what we're smelling?

Create your own eco-friendly air freshener with this crafty take on an aromatherapy reed diffuser.

Most commercially available reed diffusers use a narrow-necked bottle because that helps to keep the oil from evaporating as quickly as it would if it were exposed to more air. To make the opening on our DIY version smaller than the mouth of the Mason jar, we are going to make an insert to fit between the jar and the screw band.

1. Pour almond oil into the jar until you fill it about halfway; this will be about ½ cup. If you don't have almond oil on hand, try baby oil or safflower oil.

2. Choose your essential oil(s). If you are all about lavender, go ahead and use it straight. If you have some other scents you love, experiment with creating your own blends. I have lavender and geranium on hand. I love them both, but I find geranium to be too intense, so I opted to mix thirty drops of lavender with fifteen drops of geranium.

3. Whichever scent or blend you choose, add a total of forty-five drops of essential oil to the jar. Splash in about a teaspoon of alcohol or vodka to help the oils wick up the sticks. Gently swirl the jar around to mix the oils and alcohol.

4. The bamboo skewers should be roughly twice as long as your jar. Most skewers seem to be about ten inches long and the pint jar is 4 inches tall, so cut off about two inches from the pointy end of the skewers. Adjust as necessary based on your own personal skewers. The bamboo is pretty soft so you don't need anything fancy to cut the skewers—use sharp scissors, wire snips, or my favorite, cat claw clippers.

5. Go to the kitchen sink and hold the side of your plastic cup over the lit lighter for just a few seconds. It will melt a hole in the plastic and the edges will be nice and smooth, not like the jagged edges you would get if you cut the hole. Remove the flame as soon as this happens—you want a nickel-sized hole. Carefully use your finger to shape the hole if it isn't a nice circular opening. The plastic will still be melty and pliable but not too hot. But this all has to happen very quickly! If yours comes out bad, just try again.

6. Cut the bottom from the cup and slice it lengthwise opposite the hole. Center the original metal lid over the hole and trace around it with a ballpoint pen. Carefully cut just inside the line with an X-ACTO knife. Place plastic lid atop

TIP:

Keep out of reach of cats, as they will try to bat at the sticks! Silly cats.

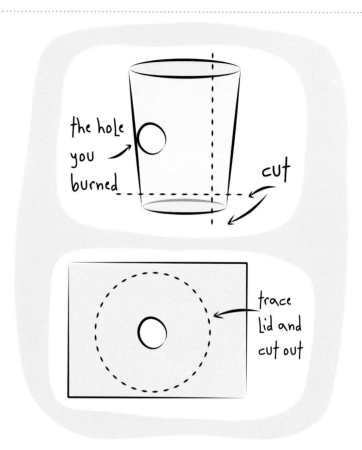

the hole you burned

cut

trace lid and cut out

the jar and screw on the band to secure it. The lip of the band will hold it in place like it does with the regular lid.

7. Dip the sticks in the oil mixture and flip them so the dipped end of the bunch is up. Place them in the hole in the jar. The oil mixture will start to slowly wick up the sticks from the bottom and soak down from the top. Smells good, right? Place in a spot that you will walk by frequently, but not somewhere that is likely to get a lot of action and commotion. After you've been using the diffuser for a while, you will notice the scent start to wane. Just flip the sticks again to refresh.

SEA GLASS JARS

omg, make your own sea glass!

"frosted glass"
spray paint
gives them that
ocean-tumbled look

You Will Need:

- Mason jars (size and quantity up to you)
- Mod Podge
- Waxed paper
- Toothpicks
- Gel food coloring
- Coffee stirrers (or something to stir glue with)
- 1-inch-wide flat artist's paintbrush
- Paper towels
- Cardboard
- Rust-Oleum "Frosted Glass" spray paint

I live on Cape Cod and even after years of beachcombing it's a thrill to find even the tiniest piece of sea glass. Imagine how beautiful a whole bottle would look filled with that frosty sapphire or emerald! Of course, it's not likely that a bottle would remain intact after years of being thrashed by nature's rock tumbler, but this project lets us fake it!

1. Disassemble the jar and set aside the lid and band for another project. Pour a blob of Mod Podge onto the waxed paper. Aluminum foil works great, too, if you don't have any waxed paper.

CRAFTY HINT

How much Mod Podge or glue you will need for a project depends on the size of the jar you are using. Start with a quarter-size blob and add more as necessary.

2. Grab a toothpick and scoop a tiny bit of the gel food coloring in your chosen color. Mix it with a coffee stirrer and add more food coloring as necessary to get the shade you want. If you got glue on the first toothpick, make sure to use a fresh one to dip back into the food coloring. You

can use one color straight or mix your own perfect shade.
Don't have any gel food coloring? No problem, you can use
the liquid stuff—you will just have to do a little bit of exper-
imenting to get the right color without making it too watery.
And if you're fussy, you might want to experiment with the
colors and let them dry on a test jar before proceeding, so
you can adjust the shade if necessary before you go painting
the whole jar. But keep in mind that you can always soak the
jar in hot water if you don't like the result, and start again.

3. When you finish mixing your color, brush it on the
inside of the jar with your flat brush. I like to start at the
bottom where the sides and base join. I find it helps to
think of it as dragging a layer of paint *on top* of the surface
(as you do when applying nail polish) rather than trying to
get it *into* the surface (as you would when applying lotion

"drag" the tinted glue across the surface

as if you are painting your nails

to your skin). Mix more paint as needed and repeat until the inside of the jar is coated. Let it dry. No, really, let it dry. You will be tempted to touch the inside to check. Wait until it dries to transparency. It will probably be uneven and streaky; if this bothers you add another coat to even it out. Let it dry again.

4. When the inside of the jar is completely dry, use a damp paper towel to clean up any Mod Podge that ended up on the outside of the mouth of the jar. Take the jar outdoors and place it mouth down on some cardboard, preferably atop a milk crate or something else to lift it off the ground. This will make it easier to get an even coat of paint. Spray the jar evenly with "frosted glass" spray paint and let it dry. Assess the level of "matte" or "frost" and if you want more, apply another coat. To get an even application and avoid drippy paint, spray slowly but don't linger too long in one spot. Let the jar dry, and then arrange it in a tableau with some sea glass and driftwood for a soothing scene.

FIRST AID JARS

* inside-outside paint job

distressed with sandpaper *

BAND-AID
sheer
strips
NEW

FIRST-AID KIT

You Will Need:

- 1 quart Mason jar with at least one smooth side
- ¾-inch blue painter's (masking) tape
- Newspaper
- Cardboard
- Wood block or milk crate
- Red spray paint
- Scissors
- White spray primer
- White gloss spray paint
- X-ACTO knife
- Sandpaper
- Spray gloss sealer (optional)
- Brown acrylic paint
- Water-based varnish such as Minwax Polycrylic

Some simple masking and an inside-outside spray paint job give life to first aid jars. Use them to store Band-Aids, gauze, and tubes of ointment, or purely as decoration in a vignette with other vintage health-care items.

1. Mask the outside of the jar by applying the painter's tape around the mouth and wrapping the rest in newspaper. Take the jar outside and set it on some cardboard atop a wood block or milk crate to lift it off the ground and make it easier to paint.

2. Spray the inside with the red paint. Let dry and repeat until you get good coverage. Remove the tape and newspaper.

3. Cut two 3-inch-long strips of painter's tape and trim all ends carefully so that they are straight. On the smooth side of the jar, place one piece of tape vertically and overlap the other on the center horizontally, forming a cross. Rub the edges of the tape down with your fingernail to ensure that it is well adhered to the jar. If you don't, the paint won't have a nice clean line.

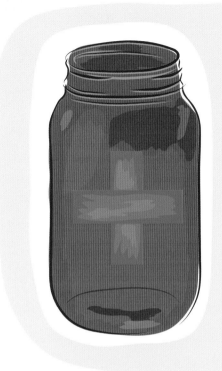

make a cross with painter's tape after you spray paint the inside red

4. Turn the jar upside down and place on the cardboard. Spray the outside with spray primer. Let it dry and repeat. When the primer is dry, spray the jar with white gloss paint.

5. Gently peel the corner of one piece of the tape off of the jar. If it seems that the paint is pulling off with it, use an X-ACTO knife to carefully score around the edge of the tape. Remove both pieces of tape completely to reveal the red cross on the inside of the jar. Clean up any rough edges of white paint with a blade.

6. Rub gently all over the outside of the jar with sand-paper. The red paint from the inside of the jar will start to show underneath the white. Use more or less pressure to get the level of distress you like.

7. Mix a dab of brown acrylic paint with some water-based varnish and paint onto the outside of the jar. Rub most of it off with a paper towel, leaving a brown tint along the mouth of the jar and at the areas of distressed paint. Let it dry. If you like, give the inside and outside surfaces a coat of spray gloss sealer to protect from unwanted scratching.

8. Fill the jar with first aid essentials or use it as a vintage-looking accent for your bathroom.

MASON FABRIC FRAMES

frame your
treasured
fabric
scraps

display
in a
group for
maximum
impact

you Will Need:

- Mason jar lids and screw bands left over from other projects
- Cardboard
- Spray primer gloss white enamel
- Chalk pencil
- Treasured fabric scraps (or some other thing that you want to frame and display in multiples, such as vintage ephemera, scrapbook papers, kids' art, cool-looking packaging, etc.)
- Thin quilt batting
- Scissors
- Glue gun

As a crafty kind of person, you probably have a bunch of fabric scraps that you adore. You are always happy to find another way to display and enjoy them instead of keeping them in a bin somewhere. Here you go: Repurpose Mason jar lids and bands into an embroidery hoop-inspired fabric display.

1. Bring the screw bands outside and lay them on cardboard, right side up. Spray them with primer and let them dry. Spray them with gloss spray paint and let them dry.

2. Using the lid as a template, trace a circle with chalk on the back of each piece of fabric that you want to frame. Lay the fabric scrap, traced wrong side up, on top of a sheet of quilt batting and pin to batting. Cut the double layer of fabric and batting about an inch outside of the traced circle.

3. Repeat this for the rest of the fabrics you will frame.

4. Place the spray-painted screw band upside down on the work surface. Place the fabric circle face down on top and lay the batting circle over that. Make sure both layers are centered over the screw band and lay the lid on top of everything.

5. Press down to push the fabric and batting toward the lip of the band. Pull both layers taut. Look at the front and smooth out any wrinkles.

6. Glue the excess fabric down to the back of the lid. If you still want to be able to use the treasured scrap later on, use low-tack masking tape to secure the fabric to itself across the back of the lid. (I do this because I know I'll want to change it after a while.)

layer as follows:

screw band

fabric, face up

batting

lid, face up

flip over and press into lid

CRAFTY HINT

Not that it matters because it will be against a wall, but if it bothers you that the glued-down fabric is unfinished on the back, you can glue down a circle of felt or card stock to cover it. If this is a gift for someone, I would do this, but if it is for my own personal use I wouldn't. I'm just not that fussy.

Move the display around on the table until you have created an arrangement that pleases you. No hanger is necessary as the frame pops right on a thumbtack, push-pin, or small nail. Hang your treasured fabric gallery.

"MERCURY GLASS" CANDLEHOLDERS

"Looking Glass" spray paint
+
mason jars
=
"mercury glass"

make several
so you have
a nice grouping
to display

You Will Need:

- Assortment of Mason jars
- Blue painter's tape
- Newspaper
- Cardboard
- Spray bottle filled with water
- Krylon Looking Glass spray paint
- Paper towel(s)
- Sandpaper (optional)
- Tea lights

All you have to do is get your hands on some Krylon Looking Glass spray paint and you can easily mimic the look of old-fashioned mercury glass. Good thing, too, because a collection of the real stuff could get expensive.

1. Mask the outside of the jar by taping around the mouth with painter's tape and wrapping the rest of the jar in newspaper. Take the jar outside and set it on cardboard.

2. Spray the inside of the jar with a few squirts of water. The water will collect into little droplets that will block the paint, creating an aged look. Spray the inside of the jar with Krylon Looking Glass paint and let it dry for a minute. Repeat twice. Let it dry completely.

3. Wipe away any remaining water with a paper towel.

4. Spray one fine coat of spray paint on the inside so the water spots aren't completely see-through. Let it dry completely and remove the tape and paper from the outside of the jar.

5. Look at the glass from the outside and decide if you want it to be more distressed. If so, rub the inside of the jar with a paper towel to remove a little more paint. If you like, you can use some fine sandpaper.

6. Put a tea light candle inside each jar. If you want to use this as a vase for flowers, remember to place a smaller glass inside and fill the glass with water, not the jar.

apply pieces
of
painter's tape
around mouth
before
painting
the inside

Ball

Mason Musings

I just love a good vignette. Treasured items can be arranged just so or haphazardly thrown together; either way, you can create a thing of beauty. Your new mercury glass Mason jars can be beautifully displayed with pretty much anything, but I love how they look when surrounded by objects with a vintage feel. Create your own tableau by collecting things you already have around the house.

Grab that old silver tea tray that never gets used and some moth-eaten doilies (or paper ones from the pantry or craft room). Maybe you have some vintage sheet music tucked in a drawer somewhere or your grandmother's perfume atomizer. Old glass buttons, a Victorian portrait, even some costume jewelry will work. A stack of old books adds height, and a scrap of velvet brings in some color and tactile interest. Add a glass full of pretty weeds from the garden or a brandy glass with a single large bloom.

Now comes the fun part: Arrange to your heart's content! Play with it. As long as you like to look at it, you've done it right.

PART 4

Fun and Festivities

Whether it's the Fourth of July and you're looking for some entertainment while grilling on the back porch or it's midwinter and the snow is flying fast and furiously outside, holidays are a great time to discover the many uses of Mason jars. With a little work on your part, these festive containers can add some crafty fun to the holidays.

MASON BUBBLE JAR

no time to make
the wand shown?
twist a pipe cleaner
into shape and
you're good to go

BUBBLES!

You Will Need:

FOR THE BUBBLE SOLUTION

- 8-ounce Mason jar
- ½ cup of water
- 4 tablespoons of liquid dish soap
- 2 tablespoons of light corn syrup (such as Karo)
- Spoon

FOR THE WAND

- 12-gauge coated aluminum floral wire, your choice of color (available at craft stores)
- Wire cutters (scissors will work in a pinch)
- Large permanent marker and pencil (to wrap wire around)
- Sandpaper or nail file (optional)
- Plastic pony bead assortment
- 12-inch piece of ½-inch-wide ribbon (per wand)

Who doesn't love bubbles? With a Mason jar and a handmade beaded wand, a magical afternoon is practically guaranteed.

The Bubbles

1. Mix the ingredients together in the jar and stir slowly but thoroughly with a spoon.

2. Test the bubbles with the wand. Depending on the soap you use, you may need to adjust the proportions a little. If the solution is too watery and bubbles won't form, gradually add a little more dish soap and corn syrup until you can easily create several bubbles with one blow. If the solution is too thick, add water in small amounts until you get plenty of bubbles.

The Wand

1. Cut a 10-inch section of wire for each wand. Aluminum wire is very pliable, so to shape the bubble end of the wand, simply use your hands. At 4 inches down from one end, bend the wire to a 90-degree angle. That short end is going to turn into the bubble-blowing part of the wand.

Hold the long part of the wire vertically, so the short part is sticking out horizontally. From the bent part of the wire (not the end) shape the short section into a nickel-sized circle around your fingers or a thick marker. You'll have wire left over that extends beyond the circle. Wrap that excess wire around the long section twice, just under the circle.

2. Snip off the remaining piece of the short section that you didn't wrap. Make sure there are no sharp edges sticking out. File the end of the wire down with sandpaper or a nail file if necessary.

3. If you have different shapes and colors of pony beads, play with different options for the beaded handle until you find a combination you like. Thread 3 inches worth of beads onto the wire.

4. Hold the wand vertically with the bubble end down. Bend the remaining wire to a 90-degree angle as you did in step 1. This time make a smaller circle by wrapping the wire around a pencil. Wrap the excess wire around the handle twice, just under the smaller circle. Again, smooth any rough edges.

5. Thread the ribbon through the small loop and tie it off. You can tie it at the base of the wand as shown, or you can tie it so the ribbon forms a loop to wrap around the wrist.

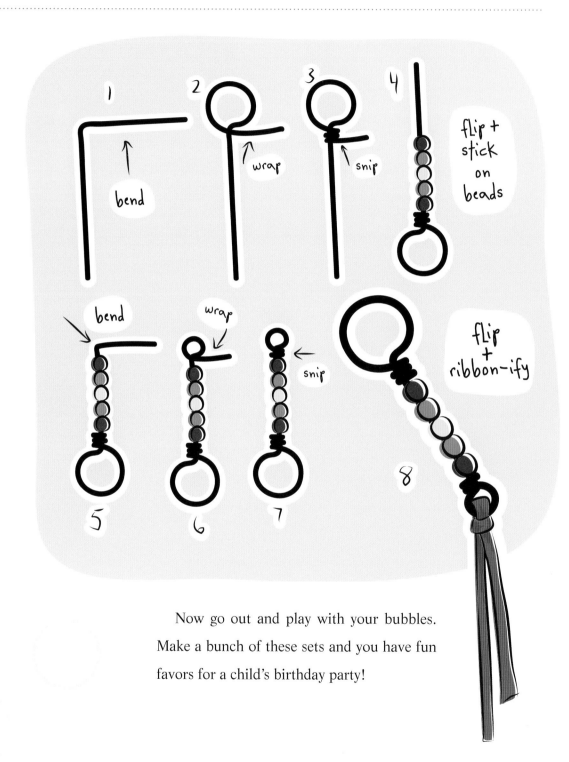

Now go out and play with your bubbles.
Make a bunch of these sets and you have fun
favors for a child's birthday party!

TWINKLE LIGHT GARLAND

these would
look amazing on a
white tree

or tuck around photos
on the mantel

You Will Need:

- 5 diamond pane jelly Mason jars (4-ounce)
- Foam core board
- Pencil
- X-ACTO knife
- Cardboard or wood block
- Dark green paint (optional)
- 1 strand of twinkle lights (green wires if using on a green tree, white if using on a white tree)

Remember those strings of Christmas lights that had the tubes of bubbling water? This project reminds me of those—a little larger and heavier than most other ornaments, but well worth the extra care to arrange and secure them on the tree. Plus, they are magic.

1. Unscrew the bands and separate the lids from the jars. Using one of the lids as a template, trace five circles onto the foam core with a pencil. Set the lids aside to use in another project.

CRAFTY HINT

If you use the metal lids in this project, they might get warm to the touch if the lights are left on. Just to be safe, use foam core instead.

2. Grab your X-ACTO knife and cut the foam core just inside of the line you traced so that the foam core circle is a bit (just a bit!) smaller than the lid. Of course, you will want to make sure you don't damage the surface under the foam, so put some extra cardboard or a block of scrap wood underneath before you start cutting.

3. Make a dot in the center of each foam circle. Use the X-ACTO blade to cut a hole at the dot just large enough for the bulbs (and plastic holders) to fit through, about ½ inch. If you make the hole too big, the lights will pop out too easily. You want it to be snug. If you find that you did make the hole larger than it should be, don't fret. Just put some masking tape on the underside of the foam circle and make a little slit in it for the bulb to go through. This will help tighten the hole a bit and the stickiness of the tape will help keep the wires in place. Just make sure the tape isn't sticking to the bulb itself, but rather on the plastic of the base.

4. Pinch around the perimeter of the foam core circles, squishing the edges a bit. If you skip this step, the band will not have room to screw closed on the jar. If you are planning to put the garland on a green tree and you want the strand to blend in with the background, you may choose to paint the foam core dark green on both sides before the next step.

5. Now it's time to assemble the garland. The number of bulbs to leave between each jar depends on the length of your string of lights. Simply look at the string and space the jars out evenly across it. Push two or three bulbs through the hole in each circle. Adjust as necessary to get the spacing as you like it. If you want more jar lights on your tree, make multiple garlands and plug them together.

6. Arrange on the tree by tucking the jars in between branches. If you like, use wire ornament hangers to help support the garland. You could also use this on a mantel with seasonal greenery and other holiday decorations to create a lovely display. This garland is for indoor use only.

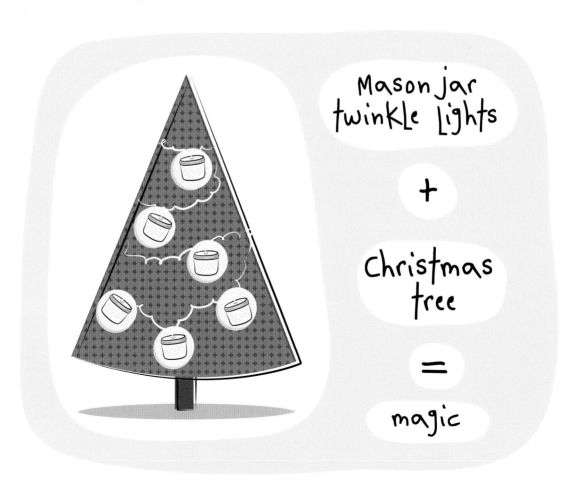

Mason jar twinkle lights

+

Christmas tree

=

magic

SPARKLE JARS

ooooh,
sparkles!

you Will Need:

- Paintbrush
- Mason jars, your choice of size and quantity
- Mod Podge
- Assortment of metallic confetti
- Assortment of glitter, super fine and medium
- Sheet of paper
- Battery-operated tea lights

Two of my favorite things, together at last: Mason jars and glitter! Use this simple project as an opportunity to get creative with different kinds of glitter and novelty confetti.

1. Using the brush, completely paint the inside of the jar with Mod Podge. Try to get an even coat, not drippy but not too thin either.

2. Choose your confetti and move it around between your fingers to break apart any clumps. Hold the jar horizontally and sprinkle a few pieces of confetti onto the Mod-Podged inside surface of the jar. Slowly turn the jar and sprinkle more until you have a smattering of confetti all over the inside of the jar. You don't want to just drop it in or it will all be on the bottom where you won't see it! If some pieces have clumped together, gently move them apart with a skewer. If you want to use another kind of confetti, go ahead and add that the same way as the first kind.

3. Next, choose two coordinating glitters, one super fine and one medium. Starting with the fine glitter, gently shake a little bit into the jar. Keep in mind that where this glitter sticks, the other one won't, so be sure to leave some room for the other kind. Shake the jar gently so any loose glitter will get caught by the Mod Podge.

4. Now, using your medium glitter, shake a bunch onto the inner surface of the jar, especially where there isn't much glitter yet. Keep adding glitter as necessary. Put the lid and band on the jar and gently shake the loose glitter around until the entire inside of the jar has either glitter or confetti on it. Open the jar and shake out any extra bits onto a clean sheet of paper. If there is enough worth saving, fold the paper and pour the glitter into a container for future use.

5. Let the jars dry for several hours. Once the Mod Podge has dried (it will go from opaque white to clear), gently tap the bottom of the jar and shake to remove any extra glitter that didn't completely stick.

6. Seal the inside of the jar with another coat of Mod Podge and let it dry before placing a battery-operated tea light in the bottom of the jar.

a recipe for awesome

Mason Musings

Festive enough for parties and cute enough for everyday use, these glittered jars can be customized for holidays or events. They are so fun and easy to make that any time is the perfect time to get your sparkle on!

Imagine sipping hot chocolate on a cold winter evening by the light of some magical candleholders of iridescent white glitter and snowflake confetti. How about some heart confetti and pink holographic glitter to set the mood for your Valentine's Day dinner? It's so easy to come up with these combinations once you get rolling: star confetti and red glitter for Independence Day, bat confetti and orange glitter for Halloween, number-shaped confetti and coordinating glitter for a young one's birthday, dove confetti and silver glitter for a bridal shower . . . you get the idea. Use your imagination and have fun.

SNOWMAN HOT CHOCOLATE GIFT JAR

make sure to keep a white dot
in the eyes so he looks alive
like Frosty

hot vanilla = yum

you Will Need:

- Mixing bowl
- ½ cup of nonfat milk powder
- ¾ cup of confectioner's sugar, sifted or with the clumps broken up
- ½ cup of finely grated white chocolate
- ½ teaspoon of salt
- Sharpie pens in black and orange, and pink (optional)
- Ball 16-ounce wide-mouth Mason jar (this is a special kind made for cute gift giving; if you can't find it, use a Kerr pint jar, because it has a smooth side you can draw on)

It's not really hot chocolate, it's hot vanilla! Finely ground white chocolate is the secret ingredient that makes this treat so amazing. Make multiple batches and you have yummy gifts to keep on hand during the holidays.

1. In a mixing bowl, combine the nonfat milk powder, confectioner's sugar, grated white chocolate, and salt. Mix thoroughly and set it aside.

To Decorate the Jar

2. Use the Sharpies to draw a snowman face on the jar. Once the jar is filled, the color of the mix will make him look white. For now you are just drawing his features. Make two eyes with your black pen, leaving a little blank square uncolored in the upper right in each "eye."

3. Draw the carrot nose in orange, and then outline it and add details with black.

4. Draw the mouth in black. You can draw a line mouth or little uneven circles as if they are rocks.

5. To make the marks more permanent and set the ink, you can bake the jar in the oven. Preheat the oven to 350°F, then place the jar on a baking sheet and put it in the oven for 30 minutes. Turn the oven off and allow the jar to cool for a while before removing it with oven mitts.

6. Once the jar is decorated and cured, fill it with the drink mix. When you're ready to enjoy your hot chocolate, heat 1 cup of milk and add ¼ cup of the mix. Stir it and devour.

Yum.

Multiply the ingredients to make larger batches for gift giving.

how to draw a snowman face

eyes:

draw 2 black circles,
leaving a white spot in each.
make little curved lines over the eyes
to give personality.

nose:

draw an elongated triangle
with a rounded base.
add a few curved detail lines.

mouth:

draw a flat bean shape.
draw short lines vertically
to define the teeth.

you just drew
a fine lookin'
snowman, friend.

VALENTINE KEEPSAKE ORNAMENT

change up the colors and you've got ornaments for any occasion

rickrack

You Will Need:

Mason jar lids—size and quantity your call

White craft glue

Paper towel

Sheet of paper

Glitter

Rickrack

Hot glue gun

Ribbon

Felt

Scrabble tiles

Card stock

Craft glue

Use some of those leftover canning jar lids to make these sweet Valentine keepsakes. Rickrack, glitter, and Scrabble tiles are what I used, but this project offers lots of opportunity for improvisation. You can change the colors and theme to make these ornaments for any holiday or occasion.

1. First we'll glitterize the lid. On the right side of the lid, squeeze out some craft glue onto the center. Using your finger, smear the glue so it covers the lid just inside the lip of the lid. With a tiny bit of damp paper towel, clean up any glue that got on the raised edge.

2. Pour on a bit of glitter and shake it around over a piece of paper to catch the overflow. Add more glitter as necessary to get full coverage on the gluey area. This leaves the pretty metallic edge, but covers up the branded writing. Let it dry completely.

3. Now it's time to add the rickrack to the back edge of the lid—the length depends on the size of your lid. Turn the raw cut edge so it is perpendicular to the lid and glue it down with hot glue. (This is so the raw edge doesn't show.) Turn the rickrack so half the length can be glued down and

the other half shows when you are looking at the right side of the lid. Glue it down a couple of inches at a time. Be careful, that hot glue is *hot*, yo! When you get to the place where you glued the beginning, turn the last raw edge in and glue down.

4. Double up a 6-inch length of ribbon and tie a knot at the bottom of the raw ends. Make a blob of hot glue on the back of the lid where the raw edges of the rickrack are and glue the knot of the ribbon in place there. Make sure the loop of ribbon is pointing to the outside of the lid as in the photo. This will be the hanger for the ornament.

5. Use another lid the same size as a template to trace a circle onto the felt. (I used a pencil, you can use whatever you like.) Cut the circle out just inside the traced line. Hot glue this circle to the back of the lid, covering the glued-on part of rickrack and loop. You shouldn't see any of this when looking at the front of your ornament.

6. Decide what you want to spell out with your Scrabble tiles and use the hot glue gun to glue down your letters. Of course, if you don't have Scrabble tiles, this is the perfect time to improvise. Maybe you'd like to use a heart cut from a paper doily, a cute love-themed button, a pretty sticker, or vintage calling card—whatever you like.

7. To finish, personalize your ornament. For a regular-size lid, cut a 2-inch-diameter circle of card stock; for a wide mouth lid, a 2½-inch circle. Write your greeting on the circle and use craft glue to adhere it to the center of the felt circle on the back of your ornament. Give as a token of love, use as a fancy-pants gift tag, or make several and display on your Any Holiday Branch Tree (coming up soon).

spell out greetings with Scrabble tiles

3-letter words on wide-mouth lids

2 letters wide on regular mouth lids

HOLIDAY PHOTO DISPLAY

display
cards
or
photos

change up
the
contents
for
each season

You Will Need:

- Drill press or hand drill
- Mason jars (I used a wide-mouth half-gallon jar and a quart-size jar)
- Wood block
- Metal file or sandpaper
- Aluminum floral wire 1/16 inch
- Twist-on wire connectors, AKA wire nuts (found in hardware stores in the electrical supplies section)
- Foam core
- Vintage glass ornaments (or something pretty to put in the jar)
- Plastic pony beads

Dress up your mantel with this decorative photo holder. It's perfect for displaying your favorite Christmas cards too.

1. Using the drill press, make a ¼-inch hole in the center of the lid. A drill press works best because it doesn't leave burrs (sharp bits of metal).

2. If you don't have a drill press, use a hand drill as follows: Drill a pilot hole with a small bit then enlarge the hole using a ¼-inch bit. If there are sharp edges on the underside of the lid, file as needed to make it smooth.

3. If you don't have a hand drill either, use a hammer and nails of increasing sizes to get the holes to about ¼ inch across. Make sure you use a block of scrap wood under the lid as you hammer the nail. File the underside of the lid as necessary using a metal file (or sandpaper if you don't have a file).

4. Find something to coil the wire around—I used one of those fat permanent markers. If it is between the diameter of a dime and a quarter, you'll be fine. Try a broom handle if you can't find anything else. It will be a little awkward, but it will work. Of course, you can just use your fingers but you get a more uniform and tight circle if you use something as a guide.

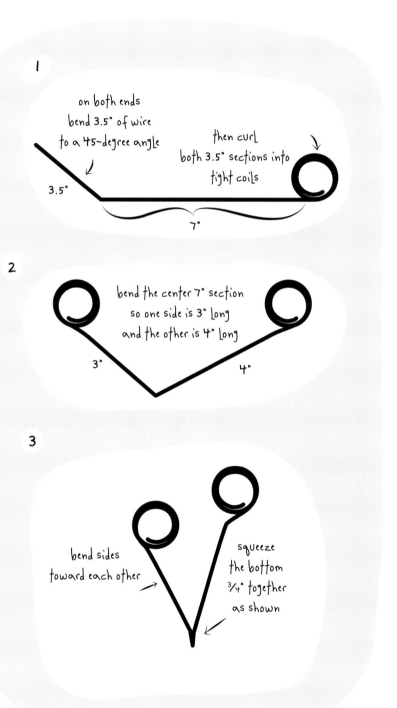

1 on both ends bend 3.5" of wire to a 45-degree angle

then curl both 3.5" sections into tight coils

3.5"

7"

2 bend the center 7" section so one side is 3" long and the other is 4" long

3"

4"

3 bend sides toward each other

squeeze the bottom ¾" together as shown

5. Start with a 14-inch length of wire and bend and coil it according to the illustration. Thread the pony bead onto the doubled length of wire as shown.

6. Place the wire stem into the hole in the lid and hold the pony bead snug to the lid as you screw the cap onto the wire on the underside of the lid.

7. Fill jar with vintage Christmas ornaments or some other pretty seasonal item. Can't think of anything? You can spray paint some pinecones or fill the jar with a few bags of peppermint candies in wrappers. Ball up one of those tinsel garlands or fill the jar with metallic bows.

8. Place the wired lid onto the jar and secure it with the screw band. Grab your favorite holiday photos or cards and tuck them into the wire coils, and you're done.

These look great in multiples across a mantel. Make them in varying heights to display several holiday cards or photos at once. Throw an evergreen swag and some twinkle lights on the mantel in between the jars and you have your seasonal display.

Mason Musings

You can easily customize this for any other holiday.

- Thanksgiving: Fill with bittersweet. Write things you are thankful for on index cards and display in the coils.
- Valentine's Day: Fill with candy hearts and show off some vintage cupid postcards.
- Halloween: Fill with toy creepy crawlies and pictures of your kids in their costumes.

You get the idea.

HOMEMADE HOODSIE CUPS

for a
perfectly reasonable size:
use a wide-mouth
half pint jar

for a
teeny-weeny size:
use a 4 oz. jelly jar

You Will Need:

- ½ gallon of vanilla ice cream
- Spoon
- Famous chocolate wafer cookies (or whatever else you would prefer to mix with your ice cream)
- Mixing bowl
- Wide-mouth half-pint jars
- Butter knife

I still get a little flutter in my heart when I think about Hoodsie Cups (as we call them in New England; you may know them as something else), those individual-sized ice creams with wooden spoons that we used to get in elementary school and at birthday parties. When I found out that you can freeze most Mason jars, I knew I wanted to make my own fancy-pants version of that childhood treat.

1. Leave the ice cream on the counter for a little while to let it soften a bit so you can mush it around easily. You'll know it's ready for doctoring when you can scrape a spoon across the top and it scoops up some ice cream rather than bending the spoon or breaking your hand.

2. While the ice cream is softening, crush half of the package of the chocolate cookies into a large mixing bowl. I like a lot of cookies in my ice cream, so I use a lot, but adjust to your preference. Of course, you can add in whatever you like instead of chocolate cookies. Maybe you'd prefer crushed gingersnaps, peanut butter cups, or pistachios.

3. Scoop out the ice cream into the mixing bowl and fold the cookies together with the ice cream.

4. Once combined, scoop the mixture into the Mason jars and level it off with a butter knife. Wipe off the outside of the jar with a damp cloth if you were messy.

5. Replace lid and secure with screw band.

6. Store the jars in the freezer until you are ready to eat the ice cream. If you have leftover ice cream, put it back in the tub the vanilla ice cream came in and freeze.

the original Hoodsie cup was created by by HP Hood in 1947

Mason Musings

You know those single-serving sundaes you can get in the frozen foods section at the grocery store? Why not make your own with your favorite flavor? Follow the previous 1–3 steps, but instead of filling the jars the whole way with ice cream, fill them two-thirds of the way. Then pour on your favorite toppings, such as chocolate sauce or caramel, and top with something else that you love, maybe crushed candy, nuts, or sprinkles. I'm a fan of salty things mixed with sweet things, so I like crushed pretzel nuggets on top! Use whatever turns you on. Put the lid on and secure with the screw band. Next time you get a hankering, your mini-sundae will be waiting for you.

GLITTER GLOBES

no water needed
for these glitter globes!

HELLO

YOU ARE CUTE

I LIKE YOU

use
alphabet beads
to spell out your greeting

You Will Need:

- Plastic figurines
- Polyester batting (available at fabric and craft stores)
- Mason jar, whatever size you like that suits the scene you create
- Hot glue gun
- Spray paint
- Fine glitter
- Cotton ball
- Felt
- Plastic alphabet beads

I wanted to reimagine the snow globe as a year-round thing, so I came up with this glitter globe. It's the perfect customizable gift for any time of year—and this one doesn't use water, so it opens up the options for what you can put inside.

1. Gather your materials and play around with them to see what kind of arrangement you like. With water-filled globes you have to worry about whether your scene elements would melt, disintegrate, rust, or otherwise get ruined in the water. This version takes away that problem, so put whatever you like inside. I like to keep it simple with a single plastic animal figurine, but you can get more complicated if you like.

2. If you have short figures, it helps to build up the lid surface to give some height. Otherwise the critters are hardly visible through the curvy neck of the jar. Ball up some poly batting into a half-ball shape. Cover the wrong side of the lid (on the inside of the rubber ring) with hot glue and carefully glue the flat-ish side of the fluff ball to the lid. Once the glue dries, take it outside and give it a few coats of spray paint to color it and firm it up.

wrangle the batting into a half sphere

before

after

3. Place your critter on the batting ball and press him in a little bit to make a place to glue his feet. Once you have made little base impressions, remove the figurine and put hot glue on him where he will come in contact with the base. Press the animal down into the base and glue him in place some more with a few blobs of glue over his feet.

4. Sprinkle some fine glitter inside the jar and shake it around—it sticks to the inside of the jar surface like magic. I used a cotton ball to gently wipe away a little oval of glitter where the front of the globe will be, so the animal is visible.

5. Gently place the decorated lid into the jar and arrange the front of the scene to be where you cleared some glitter away from the glass surface. Carefully screw on the band making sure that the scene stays put.

6. Cut a ¾ × 10-inch piece of felt for regular-mouth jars, ¾ × 12-inch for wide-mouth jars. If you like, glue some rickrack or ribbon onto the felt. Lay out the alphabet beads to spell out your greeting and hot glue them onto the felt, one letter at a time. Of course, use your imagination here and glue on anything you like, perhaps some acrylic gems or cute buttons. Use the hot glue gun to glue the felt band to the base of the jar over the screw band. Let the felt overlap on the back of the jar; glue it down and snip off any extra. Give your adorable gift to someone you love, or someone you think is cute.

TREE BRANCH CENTERPIECES

vintage sheet music makes awesome leaves

this is the perfect project for showing off your old-timey jars

You Will Need:

- Dried branches
- Garden pruners
- Cardboard
- Spray paint
- Mason jar, your choice of size
- Glass pebbles, rocks, or shells
- Vintage sheet music or some cool-looking scrapbook paper
- Double-sided tape
- Hot glue gun

There's nothing like branches to perk up a room's décor. When I bring branches inside, it makes me happy. In the spring I collect forsythia, then lilac. In summer it's sprays from the privet hedge. Fall brings bittersweet, and the year ends with holly. Try this project for a year-round option that is infinitely customizable to your taste. This is the perfect project for using your prized vintage jars.

1. Gather sticks and small branches that are no larger in diameter than a nickel. Grab whatever attracts you; you can always narrow your selection later.

2. Gently brush off any bugs before bringing the branches inside! With pruners, trim off branches from the bottom 6 inches of each stick.

3. Lay the branches on cardboard and spray paint them. Let them dry, turn them over, and repeat. Keep repeating until all of the branches are fully painted. If you find that some spots are not getting covered, prop them up in a coffee can filled with rocks and spray the hard-to-reach areas.

4. Gently use the glass pebbles, rocks, or shells to fill the jar about one-third of the way. This will add some weight to balance the sticks, as well as give the wood something to tuck into, making them more secure.

CRAFTY HINT

When I go to the beach, I like to collect what I call "beach brick" rather than rocks or shells. It's exactly what it sounds like—ocean-tumbled pieces of brick. Do you have some quirky collection you could put on display? Maybe a bunch of metal Matchbox cars, your dad's old marble collection, or even children's plastic toy animals?

5. One at a time, push the bottom of the branch into the material at the bottom of the jar. Arrange the branches to your liking. Vary the height and position of the sticks. Trim the bottom of branches that are too tall.

6. Once you get the branches arranged to your satisfaction, it's time for the leaves. Cut several simple leaf shapes from your vintage sheet music or scrapbook paper. Hold a leaf up to the branches and see where it looks right. Cut a ¼-inch piece of double-sided tape and attach the leaf to the branch. Repeat for as many leaves as you like. Rearrange the leaves until it looks good to you. Now secure the leaves to the branches with hot glue from the back.

secure the back of the leaves to the branch with a glue gun

Mason Musings

I hardly ever do a project the way I see it in a book—I always have to make it my own. I encourage you to do the same and use this project as a rough guide or inspiration for your own creative urges. If you prefer, forget about the leaves and make one of these versions:

- Beachy: If you happen to have a collection of driftwood, use that. The naturally buffed wood works perfectly with any décor. Tuck the wood into a jar filled with shells and rocks from your beachcombing.

- Glam: Paint the sticks in bright colors and use plastic gems in the bottom of the jar.

- Country: Whitewash the sticks by painting them with watered-down water-based primer such as Kilz 2. Tuck them into a jar filled with vintage clothespins or cookie cutters.

- Ethereal: Spray the branches silver and arrange them in a jar filled with semiprecious gemstones such as quartz and amethyst crystals.

- Earthy: Keep the sticks natural and fill the jar with acorns, pinecones, or seed pods.

- Christmas: Drape the branches with battery-operated twinkle lights and decorate them with vintage Christmas ornaments.

- Halloween: Spray the branches matte black and arrange them in candy corn. Decorate the display with toy spiders and snakes.

Now come up with your own variations. See, you're creative.

VINTAGE HALLOWEEN LANTERN

color in
the faces
however
you like

139

You Will Need:

* Watercolors, permanent markers, colored pencils— whatever you like to color in faces

* Photocopies of jack-o'- lantern, vampire, and Frankenstein from the Appendix

* Scissors

* Mod Podge

* Quart-size Kerr brand jars with three smooth sides

* Black construction paper (one 4½ × 12-inch piece for each lantern)

* Hole punchers in different sizes (I use a standard ¼-inch and a tiny 1⁄16-inch puncher)

* Aluminum florist's wire

* Needle-nose pliers

* Pony beads

* Glow stick, battery-operated tea light, or strand of battery-operated twinkle lights

I am crazy for vintage Halloween décor, but the real thing is hard to come by—not to mention spendy. For these lanterns, I conjured up some spooky creatures inspired by that old-timey look. Photocopy the black-and-white drawings in the Appendix and you are ready to get this (Halloween) party started.

1. Use the watercolors, magic markers, or colored pencils to color in the photocopied Halloween images however you like. If you use watercolor, you can just paint right over the top of the print without having to worry about staying inside the lines. Watercolors are translucent so the black will still show up. Do whatever floats your boat. If you don't have any watercolors handy, use colored pencils, markers, or let the kids have at them with crayons.

CRAFTY HINT

Don't feel you have to paint these guys just like I painted mine. Maybe you want to get creative with your bad self and make blue pumpkins instead of orange. Let yourself go!

2. Cut on the dotted line around each of the faces.

3. Glue the faces to the jars one at a time. Smear Mod Podge onto the back of a face and press it to the outside of the jar. Make sure you get the Mod Podge all the way to the edges so the paper adheres completely to the glass.

4. Gently smooth out any air bubbles with your fingers by pushing the bubbles outward toward the edge of the paper. Repeat with the remaining jars and pictures. Let them dry completely.

5. Punch holes randomly into the black paper. This will let the light through and create a neat pattern, so the more holes the better. Roll up the length of paper until you have a tube about the size of an empty toilet paper roll. Place it inside the jar and let go, which will allow it to unroll and expand to fit the inside of the jar. Adjust it with your fingers so the over-lapping edges are at the back of the lantern.

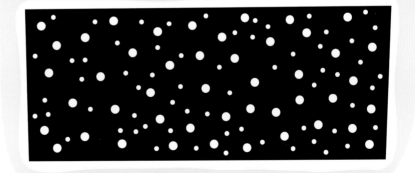

punch holes in the black paper

6. To start the handle, cut a 12-inch piece of the wire. Bend it into a U shape and use needle-nosed pliers to make a loop at one end. String your pony beads onto the handle until you have about an inch of wire left and make a loop at the other end.

7. Cut another 12-inch piece of wire and wrap it halfway around the mouth of the jar. Thread the loops of the handle you just made onto each side of the wire so that the loops are across from each other and the handle is centered on the jar. Continue wrapping the wire around the mouth of the jar and twist it together as you would with a garbage tie. Trim the wire and tuck any sharp ends in toward the jar.

8. Add a glow stick or a battery-operated tea light, or fill the jar with a strand of battery-operated twinkle lights and enjoy your spooky lantern!

LID-DLE PUMPKIN

spray-paint
whatever color
you like ➘

even better:
use rusty bands
if you have them

You Will Need:

- Canning jar lids, about 20, either regular or wide-mouth size, not a mixture
- Cardboard
- Spray paint
- Pipe cleaner
- Scissors
- Twig, about the diameter of a dime
- Aluminum florist wire
- ⅜-inch ribbon
- Hot glue gun
- Chenille, burlap, or home décor fabric scrap

I was messing around with the screw bands from some Mason jars, trying to figure out what to make, when my husband said they reminded him of a Slinky. I looked up Slinky crafts on the Internet and found that some people have made pumpkin decorations out of Slinkys, so I had to try my own Mason jar band version. Make a bunch and you've got your Thanksgiving table decorations all set!

1. Go outside and lay out all the lids right side up on a piece of cardboard. Spray-paint them whatever color you want your pumpkin to be. Let them dry, flip them over, and repeat. If you are lucky enough to have an old assortment of bands that are nice and rusty, just leave them unpainted for a junk-style pumpkin. I had an assortment of silver- and gold-tone bands, so I painted them all silver.

2. Thread the bands onto the pipe cleaner, all facing the same direction. Twist the pipe cleaner tightly to fasten, as you would with a garbage tie, and check to see if the bands form a pumpkin shape. Sometimes the first try doesn't work, so you need to loosen or tighten the pipe cleaner.

Once you have the right fit, trim the excess pipe cleaner away. Arrange the bands to your liking.

3. Audition the twig as different lengths of pumpkin stem, and cut it to your desired length (mine was 4½ inches). You can paint the twig or leave it natural, depending on your preference. I had some painted branches left over from the Tree Branch Centerpiece, so I just used one of those. If it is thick enough, you can just wedge it into the center of the bands and you're done. If you need to, wrap the bottom of the twig in burlap to give it more width and place it in the center of the pumpkin. Use the hot glue gun to glue it in place from the bottom.

4. Cut an 8-inch section of wire and twist it around a pencil to make a coil. Bend it as needed to make it look like a vine tendril. Wrap the wire with ribbon, securing it at each end with hot glue so the ribbon doesn't come undone. Tuck one end in place with the stem and use hot glue to keep it in place.

chenille scrap

cut out leaf shape

5. Cut a simple three-pointed leaf shape from chenille, burlap, or home décor fabric and hot glue it into place by the stem.

CRAFTY HINT

Other options for the stem: a bunch of cinnamon sticks, twisted-up brown craft paper, a bunch of bittersweet vines, or a real pumpkin or gourd stem.

6. Glue on whatever other bits you like: perhaps a velvet ribbon bow, or a bunch of acorns. If you are using your Lid-dle Pumpkin as a Halloween decoration, some faux cobwebs and plastic spiders would be a perfect addition!

EASTER MASONS

pony bead handle

Easter treats

Marshmallow Peep

pretty ribbon bow

cello grass
and
Jordan almonds

You Will Need:

- Aluminum floral wire 1/16-inch size
- Scissors
- Plastic pony beads
- Needle-nosed pliers
- Wide-mouth pint jar for a gift (not shown); wide-mouth half-pint jar for display (shown)
- 1/2-inch wide ribbon
- Cello or shredded paper "grass"
- Candy (tiny chocolate foil-wrapped eggs, jellybeans, etc.)
- Jordan almonds
- Marshmallow Peeps or chocolate bunnies
- Paper towel tube (for mailable version)

The cuteness of Marshmallow Peeps inspired this simple holiday project. Tuck these cuties in Mason jar "baskets" for a sweet hostess gift or tabletop display. You can even make a simplified version to mail to your favorite little bunny.

1. Cut a 12-inch piece of the wire. Bend it into an even U shape to make a handle. Use needle-nose pliers to make a loop at one end.

2. Thread the plastic pony beads on it until you have about an inch of the wire left. With the pliers, make a loop at this end.

3. Cut another 12-inch piece of wire and wrap it halfway around the mouth of the jar. Thread the loops of the handle onto each side of the wire so that the loops are across from each other and the handle is centered on the jar.

4. Continue wrapping the wire around the mouth of the jar and twist it together to join, as you would with a garbage tie. Trim the wire and tuck any sharp ends in toward the jar. Use your fingertips to make sure it feels smooth and no one will get scratched by jagged metal. If you need to, grab a nail file and smooth it down.

5. Cut a 12-inch length of ribbon, thread it through the handle loops, and make a bow around one side of the handle. Adjust the ribbon to cover the wire collar and mouth of the jar.

6. For the display version (shown), fill the jar completely with cello or paper grass and top with candies, arranging them above the mouth of the jar.

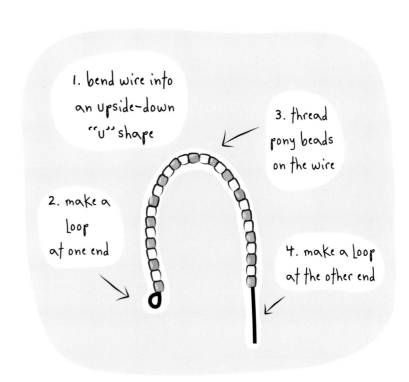

1. bend wire into an upside-down "u" shape

2. make a loop at one end

3. thread pony beads on the wire

4. make a loop at the other end

Gift Version

Stuff the cello or paper shreds into the bottom of the jar to create an inch-thick layer and follow with another inch-thick layer of Jordan almonds. Those malted chocolate eggs or jellybeans would work too, if you can keep yourself from eating all of them. Top with a Marshmallow Peep or chocolate bunny. If you can find carrot-shaped candies, those would look awesome in there. For the display version, fill completely with cello or paper grass and top with the candies, arranging them above the mouth of the jar.

Mason Musings

Are your loved ones far away? Do you want to send them a quick-and-easy Easter surprise?

Grab a quart-size Mason jar and arrange a circle of Peeps facing out at the bottom. Cut a paper towel tube to fit inside the jar vertically. Place it in the center of the jar. Stuff some cello grass between the tube and the Peeps so everything stays in place. Layer an inch of Jordan almonds on top of the Peeps around the paper towel tube. Continue layering with more Peeps and Jordan almonds until you reach the top. You will have a center tube that is empty which you can fill with more treats, toys, or a letter rolled up and wrapped with a ribbon. Any child—okay, any *human*—would love to receive something like this! Wrap it up in crumpled paper and nestle some cello grass around it. Pack the whole thing carefully and send it to your lucky bunny. Or to me.

PART 5

Useful Jars

In previous sections, you've spent some time decorating the jars and transforming them in many cases from jars to something completely different. But sometimes a jar really *is* a jar. In this section we're going to look at some things you can put in Mason jars. Of course, if you want to do a little decorating on them, that's great too!

FRUIT CRUMBLE JARS

oatmeal cookie-esque topping

make some homemade whipped cream to go on top

yumminess

you Will Need:

- 4 wide-mouth half-pint Mason jars
- Cooking spray
- Cookie sheet
- Mixing bowls
- Spoon

FOR THE FILLING:

- 2 ripe peaches, pitted and chopped
- 8 large strawberries
- Juice of 1 lemon
- 2 tablespoons flour
- 4 tablespoons brown sugar

FOR THE CRUMB TOPPING:

- ½ cup rolled oats (not instant)
- ½ cup flour
- ½ cup brown sugar
- 6 tablespoons melted butter
- ¼ teaspoon salt
- ½ teaspoon cardamom powder

The Internet told me that you can bake in Mason jars, so I had to try it. I whipped up a batch of mini fruit crumbles from some perfectly ripe peaches and strawberries and fresh-from-my-garden rhubarb. This individually portioned dessert is perfect for when you want something sweet but you know you'll eat the whole pie if you make one.

1. Preheat the oven to 325°F.

2. Spray the insides of the jars with cooking spray. Make sure you spray by the mouth of the jar because that's where the fruit will bubble up and get sticky. Place the jars on a cookie sheet.

3. In a medium bowl, combine all of the ingredients for the filling. Spoon the filling into the jars until they are almost full.

4. In a separate bowl, combine all of the ingredients for the topping. If you like, you can add some other things to it, such as some chopped nuts or different spices. Spoon it into the jars on top of the filling. If you still have some left, you can overstuff them.

5. Bake on the cookie sheet for 30 minutes or until the filling is bubbly and the topping gets a little brown. See? It's true, you can totally bake in Mason jars.

Of course, multiply the recipe as needed if you are feeding a crowd.

This recipe only makes four servings so even if you eat all of them (like I did) you're still better off than if you made (and ate) a whole pie. Right?

Mason Musings

My husband loves whipped cream. The first time I made it, I didn't put any sugar in the whipped cream. Boy, did I hear about it. After some tinkering, the following recipe was created and is deemed "Just Right." Make some for your crumble-cups.

1 16-ounce carton heavy whipping cream
⅓ cup sugar
2 teaspoons vanilla extract

    Combine all ingredients in a large, chilled metal bowl. Whip until it starts to get thick. Don't overdo it or else it will get all lumpy and buttery, and not in a good way!

    Use or refrigerate right away.

    Now go ahead and lick the beaters; you know you want to.

SPROUTING JARS

DIY sprouts!

You Will Need:

- Quart-size Mason jar
- Sharpie or other markers
- Plastic canvas
- Scissors
- Dried lentils or some other seeds
- Towel

I love salad, and I like it more when I grow what's in it. But in the wintertime my garden is bare. So I took up growing sprouts.

Healthy types say that sprouts are a nutritional powerhouse filled with vitamins and enzymes and stuff that I don't understand. What I do get is that they are fun to grow and yummy to eat, and that's enough for me. Make your own sprouting jar and go to town—it's wicked easy.

I. Most instructions for DIY sprouting call for cheesecloth. However, plastic canvas works just as well. Trace the lid of the jar onto your sheet of plastic canvas and cut out the circle. Note: The only thing about using the plastic canvas is that the holes may be too large for some of the things you want to sprout. Some of the smaller seeds will just slip right through when you are rinsing them in the jar, but lentils are perfect. If you know you will be doing lots of sprouting with small seeds, you could trace the circle onto fine stainless steel mesh if you have some. If you don't have either of these but you do have cheesecloth and a rubber band—use that!

2. Put ½ cup of lentils (or some other sprout seeds) into the clean jar, add 1½ cups of cold water, and place the sprouting lid on the jar. Let the lentils soak for half a day.

3. Invert the jar over the sink and let the water drain out. Rinse the lentils by refilling the jar with cold water and draining again. Place the jar upside down on a towel and set it someplace out of direct sunlight. Rinse and drain the lentils with cold water twice a day.

trace and cut around lid

4. Once the sprouts have developed, give them a final rinse and drain. Flip over again onto a towel and let excess moisture evaporate for a few hours. Chow down on them in a salad or refrigerate them and use them within a few days.

Experiment with different seeds, grains, and legumes to see what you like best. The basic instructions are the same for most sproutables: 1 part seeds (or nuts, or whatever) to 3 parts water. Don't get too caught up about it though. Just fill the jar with water until the level is about an inch or two above the level of seeds or whatever you are sprouting, soak 'em, and do the twice-a-day draining until they sprout.

Mason Musings

I have been seeing these jar salads all over the Internet, so I had to try them for myself. If you haven't jumped on the bandwagon yet, let me encourage you: These are so awesome. Eating a wide variety of colorful vegetables is so much easier when everything is prepped and ready to go. Even when I am not in Health Mode, I will choose salad when I open the fridge and see these beauties!

You'll need some quart-size Mason jars and chopped and grated veggies, arugula, crumbled goat cheese, and salad dressing. I like chopped red and yellow peppers, grated carrots, and beets. Feel free to mix up the methods based on your preference—slice instead of grate the carrots, julienne the peppers, etc. There's no wrong way. I mean, it's salad!

Pour the salad dressing into the bottom of the jar. Layer the veggies in a Mason jar. You can also add some of the crumbled goat cheese (if you prefer bleu, be my guest) and some fruit. My favorites are raspberries, strawberries, sliced Granny Smith apple, pistachios, candied pecans, Craisins or golden raisins, and sprouts.

Top the whole thing with arugula and a light dash of salad dressing (see the Mason Salad Dressing Mixer project for a recipe to make your own salad dressings).

Replace the lid and store the jar in the fridge for up to four days.

Note: If you know you will be grabbing a jar "to go" and will want to eat straight from the jar, leave a little more room at the top to allow the vegetables to disperse and mix when you shake the jar.

CUTE POTTED SUCCULENTS

aloe pup

pot up
a bunch
and you've got a
thoughtful
housewarming
gift

jade

christmas
cactus

You Will Need:

- 8-ounce Mason jelly jars— as many as you have cuttings for

- Drainage material to put in the bottom of the jar (rocks, marbles, even small plastic toys)

- Potting soil, dampened

- Succulent houseplants to take cuttings from (aloe, jade, burro's tail, Christmas cactus)

Make up a little tray of a few different kinds of succulent cuttings and give them to a new homeowner or someone who's living on her own for the first time. Even people with a black thumb can grow succulents!

1. Fill each jar one-third of the way with your chosen drainage material. Get creative with it! You don't have to go the normal route with pebbles, you know. The beauty of potting up your cuttings in Mason jars is that you can see through them, so make it interesting.

CRAFTY HINT

Because Mason jars don't have drainage holes in the bottom like normal planters do, it's important to add this few inches of something inorganic for drainage. If you filled the jars completely with soil, the water would soak the bottom few inches of soil and rot the roots of your new plant. A layer of rocks (or whatever your imagination conjures up) on the bottom ensures that the soil can drain freely, keeping the roots happy and slime-free. Glass, stone, and plastic are perfect materials for drainage because they won't soften or decay from sitting in the water.

2. Fill with damp potting soil until only about an inch of space is left at the top of the jar.

3. Take the cuttings as follows:

- Jade and Burro's Tail: Gently break off a 3–4 inch stem piece that has some leaves on it. Pull any leaves off the bottom 2 inches of the cutting.
- Aloe: Aloes make baby plants all on their own! These little offshoots are called "pups," and you can just twist them off the mother plant.
- Christmas Cactus: Simply snip off a length of 2 or 3 joined segments.

Don't worry too much about how to take the cuttings—if a piece breaks off and you stick it in some dirt, it will do just fine. That's the thing I love about succulents: They want to live.

4. If you have some rooting hormone lying around, feel free to dip the stripped end of the cuttings in it, but these plants propagate so easily it's not really necessary.

5. If you are patient, you can let the cut end of the cuttings dry out for a couple of days on a windowsill. If you are like me, you'll want to tuck them in the soil right away so you can enjoy how cute they look. They will be just fine if you do. Insert each cutting into its own jar, about 1½ inches into the soil. Gently press the soil around the cutting to firm it and keep the plant in place.

Bottom heat helps with growth, so you can put them on the counter above the dishwasher or dryer for a little extra oomph. The potting mix should be allowed to dry between waterings, but don't starve the poor things. Pretty soon you will see little baby leaves growing! Yes, it's really that easy.

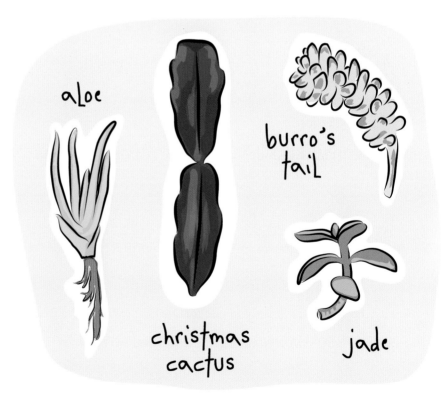

aloe

burro's tail

christmas cactus

jade

INDIVIDUAL SUN TEAS

individual-size sun teas are perfect for a
cookout or garden party

You Will Need:

- Pint-size Mason jars—as many as you want
- Same amount of tea bags

You can practically bottle summertime with these single-serve Mason jars of sun tea! Make a bunch in advance for a garden party and put them in a big bucket with some ice. Your guests can grab their favorite flavor and doctor it up just the way they like it.

1. Fill the jars with water. Leave an inch or so at the top so you have room to add ice or milk later.

2. Put one tea bag in each jar and close the lids.

3. Leave outside in the sun until the tea brews and the water changes color.

4. To make concentrates, instead of one tea bag per jar, use six. Then, remove the tea bags and put the concentrate in the fridge. When you are ready for a nice glass of iced tea, simply combine ¼ cup of the concentrate with 8 ounces of water and some ice.

5. If you made the individual servings to be enjoyed that day, you can leave the tea bag in the jar so you know which kind of tea it is. Add honey, milk, lemon slices, or ice if you like. Feel free to mix it up and use unexpected teas. Earl Gray sun tea? Sure, why not?

summer time

calls for

iced tea

tea time

If you want to get fancy, copy some of the blank labels from the Appendix onto card stock. Cut out on the dotted lines and punch a hole in each one. Use your cutest hand lettering to write the different kinds of tea. String a pretty ribbon or baker's twine through the hole and tie around the necks of the jars.

Make sure to have some simple syrup on hand (see following) to add sugar without the dreaded granular clump at the bottom.

Mason Musings

Mix your tea up even more—try 50 percent tea and 50 percent juice of your choice. One of my favorite drinks in the world is served at a charming little hobbit-hole of a restaurant—the inside of the place is made from salvaged barns! I don't know the exact recipe, but it is part black tea, part hibiscus tea, and part orange juice, and sweetened with honey. Go ahead and make up your own magical drinks. There are no rules.

To make simple syrup, mix half a cup of sugar and half a cup of water together in a saucepan and bring to a boil. Turn heat to low and simmer while stirring until the sugar is completely dissolved. Remove from heat and let cool. Pour into a jar and keep in the fridge. It stays good for about a month.

Simple syrup is perfect for sweetening those cool summer staples, iced tea and coffee, but many fun mixed drinks call for it as well. You could even add some spices to the sugar water while it's boiling to flavor your simple syrup. Try cardamom or anise seeds, but make sure to scoop them out of the syrup before putting in drinks.

APPENDIX

Halloween
Faces

Labels and
Gift Tags

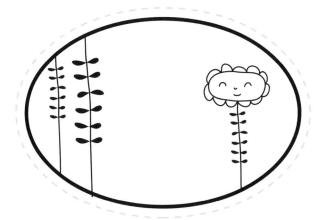

to:

from:

TO:

FROM:

Labels for Your Magnets

cut on the dotted line

go for a run

chug some water

call a friend

eat your veggies

you = awesome

take some deep breaths

INDEX